THE POCKET
ENCYCLOPEDIA OF
AGGRAVATION

THE POCKET ENCYCLOPEDIA OF AGGRAVATION

The counterintuitive approach to de-stressing

97 Things That Annoy, Bother, Chafe, Disturb, Enervate, Frustrate, Grate, Irk, Jar, Miff, Nettle, Outrage, Peeve, Rile, Stress, Trouble, Vex, & **** **You Off!**

LAURA LEE
Illustrated by LINDA O'LEARY

Hachette UK Company
www.hachette.co.uk

Originally published by Black Dog & Leventhal Publishers, Hachette Book Group,
1290 Avenue of the Americas, New York, NY 10104
www.hachettebookgroup.com
www.blackdogandleventhal.com

First published in Great Britain in 2017 by Cassell, a division of
Octopus Publishing Group Ltd, Carmelite House, 50 Victoria Embankment,
London EC4Y 0DZ
www.octopusbooks.co.uk

Design by Red Herring Design
Cover design by Carlos Esparza

ISBN 978 1 84403 982 1

A CIP catalogue record for this book is available from the British Library.
Printed and bound in China
10 9 8 7 6 5 4 3 2 1

Commissioning Editor Romilly Morgan
Senior Editor Alex Stetter
Junior Designer Jack Storey
Senior Production Manager Peter Hunt

CONTENTS

**'I said to myself, Arlo, if you were dead,
a lot of the stuff that pisses you off
probably wouldn't bother you so much.'**

—Arlo Guthrie, introduction to the song 'Wake up Dead'

INTRODUCTION

It has been more than 15 years since that August afternoon when the idea for a book bit me on the leg. I was sitting beside a pond, lazily contemplating the way the sun reflected off the ripples in the water, when my reveries were interrupted by the itchy poke of a mosquito boring into me with her sipper. My mind was filled with questions. Why do mosquitoes flock to me more than to other people? What makes that lump appear on the skin? What makes it itch? Why are there annoying things like mosquitoes on the planet, anyway? It occurred to me that other people must wonder about this kind of thing as well. Why do I keep losing socks in the wash? Why am I always in the slowest queue at the supermarket? Is there a correct answer when the policeman asks, 'Do you know how fast you were going?'

I did not know, at that moment, that I was about to write my most successful book, and that 18 or so books later I would never surpass it in sales. (Annoying!) Who knew that pet peeves could be so profitable? It seems there is something gratifying in the realization that other people have been bugged by these little occurrences and even more gratifying to know why they happen. (Not as gratifying as were they not to happen in the first place, mind you, but gratifying nonetheless.)

People are frustrated by thousands of little things, from hangnails and paper cuts to the mother of all aggravations – telemarketers, who are, incidentally, making a comeback. When the futurists of days gone by imagined a brave new world full of robots, they never dreamed these advances in technology would be used to call you in the middle of dinner to sell you something. It seems nearly every step in the march of human progress lands in dog doo.

No one is immune. On several occasions, the experts I consulted – scientists with long titles and multiple PhDs – ended our conversation by ranting about those little threads that hang from sweaters, people chewing on pencils and fitted sheets that don't.

For example, I contacted Dr Ron Grassi, DC, MS, DABDA, FACFE, Diplomate American Boards of Forensic Medical Examiners & Physical Disability Analysts, with a question about why stiff necks hurt so much. (An entry which, incidentally, did not make the final cut. Sorry about that.) Along with my answer I got the following: 'Why do people scream on mobile phones like they're yelling across a canyon? They don't do this on a regular phone. How about someone scraping the ice cream bowl with a spoon (after there is hardly any left) while you're lying in bed at night watching a movie. And the DOOR SLAMMERS!!!!! Do you know how insulting that is to a Corvette convertible?'

Other experts were not as amused by the concept. A representative of Rensselaer Polytechnic Institute seemed a bit annoyed when I phoned to ask if there was a mechanical engineer who could explain why a handheld can opener slides off the rim, leaving that little bit of joined metal that you can't seem to cut through when you start with the opener again. (I never did get an answer to that one.) One local librarian was confused when I came in and explained that I was looking for the psychology books because I wanted to find out why two pedestrians trying to get out of each other's way both dodge in the same direction, then both dodge to the opposite side and end up doing an odd pavement dance. 'You're not going to find any books on that,' she said with a squint that clearly indicated she was sure I was insane or making fun of her, or both.

In my original introduction, I wrote that we should be optimistic about the fact that we are obsessed with the dust on our computer monitors and the amount of legroom on planes. You can only muster the energy to get upset about these things when the outer world is in a state of relative peace, tranquillity and prosperity. Although I have not found statistics to back it up, my guess is that scientists spend much less time and energy trying to figure out the exact chemical composition of intestinal gas or how long it takes a biscuit to turn to mush in your mug when the nation is in the midst of war, famine, plague or economic depression. In the absence of a huge national crisis, we have the freedom to ponder the little things. In that spirit, this is a highly uplifting work. That's what I wrote just before my book came out – in the week of 11 September 2001.

Given my reasonable hypothesis, I was sure *The Pocket Encyclopedia of Aggravation* was destined to disappear without a trace. But we returned to life and laughter and, importantly for me, complaining about the little things that get on our nerves. There is no escape from aggravation. People who live and work in cities deal with smog, long queues, traffic jams, noise, crowds and an ever-more fidgety, tension-filled lifestyle. People who live in the country have their own annoyances: insects, roadkill, stepping in cow dung and having to drive 20 minutes to get to the nearest post office. Some people choose to work in offices, where they deal with difficult co-workers and bosses, uninspiring environments of office cubicles, and having to plan months in advance to get days off. Others avoid those hassles by being self-employed. They deal with self-employment tax and not having a regular salary. People who live alone have to pay all the rent and there's no one at the house to call for help if the car breaks down. People who live together have to compromise more. I have come to the conclusion that the key to life is choosing which annoyances you prefer to deal with and adjusting your lifestyle accordingly.

Annoyances are subjective, I know. I once worked as a mime. One person's noise is another's symphony. One person's aromatherapy is another's loud perfume. I compiled my original list of annoying things from personal observation and suggestions from friends and acquaintances. If I had written entries for all the items on my master list, it would rival the *Oxford English Dictionary* for shelf space. For some reason, my publisher thought that might make it hard to sell. I reduced the list by focusing on the aggravations that seem to elicit the most venom, and those that have the most interesting explanations.

Over time, however, *The Pocket Encyclopedia* had become a bit stale. In the intervening years, the word 'cyber' went from futuristic to old-fashioned; they decided to take the hyphen out of the word email; and the jury is still out on whether or not to capitalize Internet. We managed to make it through an entire decade without ever coming to a consensus about what to call it. The Noughties? The 2000s? The Aughts? CDs skipping, the laser pointer fad and VCR clocks that flash 12:00 because you can't figure out how to set them lost their power to drive us nuts. A recent study concluded that men no longer hog the television remote control. We have reached a golden age of remote control parity . . . just as we are starting to watch videos on devices other than televisions. Beginning in 2009, a law in the United States reduced the number of hidden fees and penalties that credit card companies can charge. The amount of luggage that gets misrouted by airlines has been significantly reduced thanks to better computer tracking systems.

There were even aggravations that came and went before I could document them. For example, the iPhone was introduced and it came with pre-installed apps you were not allowed to delete. So you had to put them in their own special folder called 'Apple Junk' that you hid on the fifth screen. (I'm talking to you, Stocks!) In 2016, Apple finally decided to let you delete them, and a decade from now no one will remember they ever annoyed us in that way. I have confidence, however, that Apple will find new ways. (This is, after all, the company that removed the headphone jack and sold you an expensive dongle to replace it, calling it a brave innovation.)

On a personal note, since the last edition of this book, I've come to know the frustration of having your reading glasses always in the other room. You see, botheration is a constant. The inhabitants of Teletubbyland that we loved to hate in the 1990s were replaced with Pokémon Go. Cassette tapes that unwind and get eaten by the machine and video rental late fees may be things of the past, but they were replaced with buffering delays, selfie sticks and a whole host of social-networking woes. Ten years from now, there will be something new, wondrous, consequential and full of unforeseen side effects.

Before we get to the main event, I want to take a moment to address one of the frequent complaints of grammar purists who gripe about such things in their blogs. There are those who feel that 'aggravation' is the wrong word to describe life's little frustrations. Aggravation, they say, is *making something worse.* Indeed, this is the first definition of the word. Using aggravation to mean irritation or annoyance is, however, an accepted usage. If you don't think it ought to be, you've been outvoted by the people who write dictionaries. So there! For some reason, I'm not as much on board with dictionary authors' decision in 2013 to include the popular use of the word 'literally' to mean not something that is actually true but literally its opposite (as in 'My head literally exploded').

On the subject of linguistic annoyances, one thing that has not changed since the first edition is that an inordinate number of vexations seem to start with the letter 'C'. What are you going to do?

Brain
processing
complicated
concepts

Unintelligible prose

ACADEMIC LANGUAGE

The sentence 'Since thought is seen to be "rhizomatic" rather than "arboreal", the movement of differentiation and becoming is already imbued with its own positive trajectory' appears in *The Continental Philosophy Reader*, edited by Richard Kearney and Mara Rainwater. The line is part of an introduction intended to help students understand the chapter. Sure. That explains it.

Why do academics insist on writing in language that makes the reader squint and develop a headache? It is simply a matter of style, say defenders of dense, challenging prose. Different forums have different rules. *People* magazine has a different style than the *New York Times*, which has a different style than a mail-order catalogue. Every profession has its jargon. Academic specialities have more than their share because they are expressing complicated and often new ideas.

'There's a kind of presumption among journalists and people who talk about culture in the media that if it's written by an English professor, it should be comprehensible to others,' Dr Eric Mallin, an associate professor in the English Department at the University of Texas at Austin, told the *Dallas Morning News*. 'That's assuming there is no specialized knowledge particular to the field.'

Dr Judith Butler, a professor at the University of California at Berkeley, was unwittingly thrust into the centre of the academic writing debate when the New Zealand publication *Philosophy and Literature* awarded a 90-word sample of one of her articles the top prize in its annual Bad Writing Contest. The 'honour' is given to the most 'stylistically awful sentence' to come out of the scholarly world.

Butler defended her style of writing in a *New York Times* editorial piece. Academic writing needs to be 'difficult and demanding', she said, in order to question concepts that are so ingrained no one thinks to question them. Having to think about the meaning of each sentence provokes new ways of looking at a familiar world.

Others believe the jargon has little to do with communication. They see it as something akin to a secret handshake or a series of multisyllabic passwords. It is written to confirm academic authority, membership in the club.

In 1996 a New York University physicist submitted an article with fake phrases and gibberish to the journal *Social Text*, which published it as genuine scholarly analysis. When an English professor at Southern Oregon University was asked to paraphrase a long sentence from the Bad Writing Contest's second-prize winner, he admitted, 'It doesn't make a lot of sense to me.'

Yet to gain a permanent position, professors must publish, and to be published, they must adopt the accepted style. Philosopher Bertrand Russell summed it up in his essay 'How I Write'. 'I am allowed to use plain English because everybody knows that I could use mathematical logic if I chose,' he wrote. 'I suggest to young professors that their first work should be written in a jargon only to be understood by the erudite few. With that behind them, they can ever after say what they have to say in a language "understood of the people".'

ACNE

When you reach that special age when you start to think about trying to attract a boyfriend or girlfriend, you become preoccupied with your appearance – and then Mother Nature reveals she has a sick sense of humour. Your skin begins to change, an oily sheen covers your face and pimples pop up everywhere. What is more, the stress of having acne can give you acne!

The tendency to get acne is inherited. Males are more prone to it than females during their teenage years, but because it is hormonally triggered, adult women often have outbreaks of acne that correspond with their menstrual cycles. Scientists speculate that this side effect of puberty once had a purpose. In the days when people hunted and foraged for food in the wild, the skin may have needed extra protection from the elements as we reached adulthood. Now the overactive oil glands just give you spots.

Androgens, the sex hormones released at puberty, cause the production of sebum, the fat that naturally keeps your skin and hair soft. Somehow, though, the sebum gets trapped along with dead skin cells. The follicle stretches outwards and a bump forms on top. Contrary to popular belief, blackheads are not caused by dirt that gets stuck in a pore. Blackheads are oil plugs that have made their way to the surface and turn dark when the air hits them. If they are covered and can't break through the surface, the oil plug stays white.

When the sebum in the blocked gland is transformed into free fatty acids they become food for bacteria. The body responds by sending white blood cells to kill the intruders. The result is pus and a big spot.

The tendency to get acne couldn't come at a worse time in life. David Elkind, who studied egocentrism in adolescence, showed that during our teen years we become preoccupied with our self-image. We feel there is an imaginary audience watching our every move – an audience full of critics. Stress – having a big exam, a job interview, a big date or an outbreak of acne at a time when you feel especially self-conscious – causes your body to release more androgens, which can trigger new pimple outbreaks, which can cause more stress, which causes your body to release more androgens, and so on and so on.

Girl just before the party

Epidermis

Acne

Sebum

Hair follicle

ECONOMY CLASS

Seatback fully reclined

71-79cm
(28-31in)

AEROPLANE LEGROOM, OR THE SEAT BACK IN YOUR FACE . . .

You're in the middle seat. Your bag is stowed under the seat in front of you, which means you can't stretch your legs out – unless you call putting your tootsies a couple of inches forwards 'stretching'. Your neighbours have taken both armrests and now the guy in the seat in front of you decides to lean his seat all the way back. Your thimble-sized cup of coffee is now on your lap, and you have about as much freedom of movement as a body in a coffin.

Travel, for those of us back in the steerage class, is uncomfortable and psychologically stressful because other people are planted well within our bounds of personal space. 'Quite frankly, I don't think this issue would even exist if we passed a law that required all executives of the nation's airlines to fly in the middle seat on coach,' said former Alaska Senator Frank Murkowski.

The Federal Aviation Administration (FAA) does have regulations as to the configuration of the seats on American aeroplanes. They must be designed to ensure that all passengers can exit an aircraft in an emergency within a specified period of time. There are no regulations that assure minimum comfort. To make matters worse, airlines are fuller than they've ever been. Throughout most of the twentieth century they flew with loads of 50 to 60 per cent. Ten years ago load capacity rose to 70 per cent. Now it is 84 per cent. And the airlines keep inventing new ways to shoehorn us in.

Until the 1980s the distance between your seat back and the one in front of you was 86cm (34in). When the first edition of this book came out in 2001, I reported that carriers had cut that down to 79 or 81cm (31 or 32in). Today airlines routinely provide between 71 and 79cm (28 and 31in). As travel writer Scott McCartney put it, 'one passenger's nose may be three inches closer to the back of the head in front of her.' Some psychologists believe what's going on at eye level stresses us out more than any lack of legroom.

A

That is not to say the other parts of your anatomy are comfortable in an airline seat. According to Kathleen Robinette, who studies body measurements for the US Air Force, the design of the seats has always been faulty. Sometime back in the 1960s designers opted to base the width of the seat on the average dimension of male hips. They assumed, that as men are larger than women, a seat that fitted a man would fit a woman as well. There are two problems with this. First, the shoulders and arms are wider than the hips, so your backside fitting into the seat does not prevent you from rubbing against your neighbour or spilling out into the aisle. Second, women's hips are wider than men's. So seats never quite worked for everyone to begin with. The result, Robinette says, is that the seats were about 12.5cm (5in) too narrow in the 1960s. In the 1970s and 1980s average seats were between 46 and 51cm (18 and 20in). These days they are 42 and 44.5cm (16½ to 17½in) even though the average American gained 13.5kg (30lb) and increased his hip size to 52.5cm (20$\frac{2}{3}$in) in the same time period. So bigger passengers, smaller seats. But here's the thing: as much as we love to complain about the lack of legroom, unpalatable airline food and having to pay for movie headsets (come on, I paid £300 for this ticket and you can't give me a headset for free?), we want our travel to be cheap. We buy airline tickets by going online and seeking out the lowest price. If the booking sites provided an option to search by legroom and other amenities, perhaps we would shop that way. This would make sense in the new world of à la carte pricing, but so far none of them does. Until that changes, to get our economy-class business, airlines are in a race to the bottom to offer the cheapest ticket. You can, however, do a bit of research on your own using a site like SeatGuru.com, which shows the specific jet and the configuration in each section.

ALUMINIUM FOIL AGAINST DENTAL FILLINGS

You sit down to lunch at the office and carefully unwrap a ham sandwich from a sheet of aluminium foil. Unbeknown to you, a small piece has remained in the sandwich and when you bite into your lunch the foil is pressed between your fillings. A sharp pain vibrates through your teeth, as if a sadistic dentist were trying to inspire a Pavlovian fear of ham sarnies. The pain is literally an electric shock.

This happens when you have traditional dental fillings made of mercury combined with either tin or silver. The aluminium foil acts as an anode, the filling as a cathode and your saliva is an electrolyte 'salt bridge'. The result is a galvanic cell, which releases an electrical current of up to 2 volts. Believe it or not, at least one researcher says chewing on tinfoil is good for you. According to the Wireless Flash News Service, researcher Miklos Gombkoto of the Hungarian Dental University of Györ, did a month-long study in which 20, presumably broke, Hungarian college students agreed to chew aluminium foil for 30 seconds, three times a day, for £50. Gombkoto reported that the electrical charge helped kill germs in the mouth that cause bad breath and tooth decay. Feel free to experiment on your own.

Aluminium foil

Nerve endings

Current up to 2 volts

Ants follow trail of
9-oxy-2-decenoic acid
secreted by the first
ant on the scene.

ANTS

See also *Fleas, Flies, Gnats and Midges, Mosquitoes*.

Ah late spring. The flowers grow once more, the sun shines . . . and your kitchen is suddenly swarming with ants. They're everywhere, and they just keep coming.

Why do ants suddenly appear in such large numbers in warm weather? Over the winter ants stay in their underground nests. They subsist on the stores of food they collected over the summer. When it gets warm, the population swells and the workers head out once again to collect nourishment. A crumb that is barely noticeable to a human is a tasty feast for an ant.

Most of the ants you see indoors are female workers who live in colonies outdoors. If you observe them for long, you will see that they are marching to and from a food source and carrying nourishment out of your home back to the queen. When a worker ant comes across food, she starts secreting pheromones from an abdominal gland. Other ants follow the scent and reinforce it with their own trails. As the food is exhausted, the ants stop secreting and the trail dries up. They are so guided by the scent that, if you were to wipe your finger across it and create a break in the path, the ants travelling in both directions would come to a complete stop.

Poisonous sprays are strangely satisfying, but they don't work in the long run. You get to see a few worker ants fall on their backs and die, but the poison never makes it back to the queen. As soon as their friends find the way back, you'll see ants again.

There are other reasons to avoid sprays. As many as 500 species of the most common household insects are now resistant to many of the most widely used insecticides, according to Sheila Daar, executive director of the Bio-Integral Resource Center in Berkeley, California. They can still be dangerous to humans, especially children.

Ant traps work by offering a supply of poisoned food in a dosage small enough to make it back to the nest. If the baits are too strong and you see dead ants around it, leave them where they are; eventually, other ants will take their corpses back to the nest where they will poison the colony. Dead ants have their own pheromone, 10-octadecenoic acid. Ants treat a dead peer as if it were living until they smell the acid. Then they take the body to the dead ant dumping ground. If you put the acid on a living ant, the other ants will pick it up and dump it as well. The discarded ant will return only to be carried off again until the acid evaporates.

Instead of spraying, see if you can work out where the ants are coming from. You can block the entry with a glob of petroleum jelly or toothpaste. Then clean up their path with soapy water. This will eliminate the chemical trails the scouts left for other workers.

ARMREST WARS

See also *Inefficient Pavement Pass, Standing Too Close.*

ou're next to a big man on a long plane journey. The insensitive, space-hogging guy has his oversized limb on the armrest. This is completely rude and unfair because you want the armrest to yourself. Without making eye contact, you wedge your elbow behind his. With each bump, you try to jostle your arm a little bit further forward, but his arm has become as stiff as a board. No way is he giving up. His muscles may cramp up, but his hairy forearm is going to be on that armrest until someone pries it off.

Psychologists call the areas of disputed personal space 'ambivalent zones'. Whether or not you get into a confrontation depends on who is sitting in the adjoining seat. Our bubble of personal space expands or contracts depending on how we feel about the other person. If it's a friend, family member or someone you're attracted to, you probably won't have a problem.

When it is a stranger, however, the battle lines are drawn. We rarely come to blows over the invasion, or even discuss it. We just reposition ourselves and try to slide our arm into the space. This is because we react to personal space violations by trying not to acknowledge the invader as a person.

When you ask ethics experts, as an enterprising reporter at the *Wall Street Journal* did in 2011, they were largely in agreement that the person in the middle seat deserves both armrests in compensation. The unofficial rule is: middle seats, two armrests; aisle seat, outside armrest; window seat, armrest near the wall.

This is how we generally agree it is supposed to work. It is not what we do. If the research done on this in the 1980s still holds (it doesn't appear that there has been a more recent follow-up), when a man sits beside a woman, odds are five-to-one that he will take the armrest. Dorothy M Hai and her team from the St Bonaventure University School of Business observed men and women on commercial airline flights

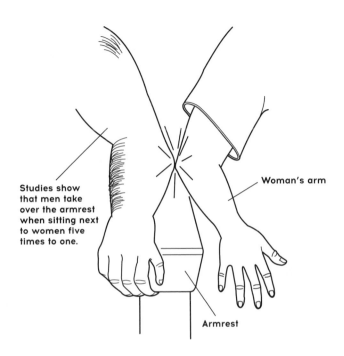

Studies show that men take over the armrest when sitting next to women five times to one.

Woman's arm

Armrest

and found that a man takes up more space regardless of whether he is bigger or smaller than the woman.

The researchers followed up by interviewing about one hundred of their subjects. They learned that travellers were fully conscious of the elbow war, even if they behaved as if they weren't.

Perhaps we should be grateful, ladies. In 2014 Auburn University microbiologists James Barbaree and Kiril Vaglenov removed materials used in planes, put them in environments that mimic flight conditions and found that deadly germs can last for up to a week on the armrest. So go ahead and let him have it.

BAD BREATH ▶ BUREAUCRACY

BAD BREATH

See also *Aluminium Foil against Dental Fillings.*

B reath test: Do people recoil when you exhale? Have you bought stock in Listerine? Do you spend more than 10 per cent of your income on mints? Does the dog run away? Has your breath killed small houseplants? You could be one of the estimated 35 to 45 per cent of the world's population plagued by bad breath, also known as halitosis or fetor oris.

'Bad breath is a problem that originates in the mouth,' Dr Jon Richter told *Men's Health* magazine. It seems obvious enough, but lately a slew of television ads have promoted pills that supposedly fix your breath problem from the inside out. They don't work. Ditto the billions of pounds a year we spend on mouthwashes, breath mints, sprays and gums. Those will reduce the odour for an hour at best.

You probably don't like to think about it, but your mouth has an ecosystem all of its own. To a micro-organism, your mouth's 36°C (95°F) temperature and high humidity is like a Hawaiian paradise. More than 400 different species call it

Bacteria coating on tongue ferments protein that releases the foul-smelling hydrogen sulphide.

With high humidity and a temperature of 36°C (95°F), the mouth is the perfect climate for microorganisms.

B

home. You feed them every day when you feed yourself. Some of the sugar and carbohydrates stay behind, providing a bacterial feast.

The tongues of some people become coated with bacteria that ferment proteins. The fermentation process produces methylmercaptan, fatty acids, ammonia and hydrogen sulphide. This last gas is responsible for the sulphur odour of bad breath. (A similar fermentation process takes place in the intestines: see *Farts*.)

No matter how much you brush and floss, your morning mouth probably smells more of sulphur than spearmint. Overnight the microorganisms that inhabit your mouth have several hours to eat and break down food into amino acids and peptides with their stinky by-products unmolested by a toothbrush.

Even if you refrained from brushing for the same number of hours during the day, your breath would not smell like it does in the morning. During the day you talk, chew and swallow. These activities help keep the saliva flowing.

Saliva, it turns out, is pretty amazing stuff. It keeps the ecosystem in your mouth in balance. It contains bicarbonate ions that buffer the tooth-decaying acids produced by bacteria like *S. mutans*. It also contains phosphate and calcium ions, which repair microscopic cavities. It is full of antibacterial agents and proteins that cause bacteria to stick to one another so they can't stick to the surface of the tooth. The saliva then washes the bacterial clumps away.

During the night, saliva production drops off and its antibacterial action stops as well. The organisms multiply, coat your tongue and wait for you to get up and grab your toothbrush.

If you seem to have foul breath no matter how much you brush, you probably have what dentists call a 'geographic tongue'. This means your tongue has more indentations than other people's. This gives anaerobic bacteria extra places in which to live and multiply.

The best way to keep your breath fresh is to clean the back of your tongue. You don't need to buy a fancy tongue cleaner – use an inverted spoon to gently scrape the back of the tongue then rinse.

Coffee

Mathematical
formula describing
rate of hot liquid
breaking down starch
and sugar in biscuit

Biscuit

$$L^{\Sigma} = \frac{\gamma Dt}{4\eta}$$

BISCUIT MUSH AT THE BOTTOM OF YOUR MUG

See also *Coffee Spills, Rustling Sweet Wrappers.*

Biscuits taste great when they're dunked in hot tea or coffee, but leave them in the liquid too long and they crumble and end up as tasteless sludge at the bottom of your mug, depriving you of your treat and ruining your morning pick-me-up. McVitie's studied the phenomenon and determined that about one-quarter of the biscuits that are dunked into hot liquid end up as glop. In the process, it splashes coffee in your face and all over your clean white shirt. Try to retrieve the biscuit and you scald your fingers, spill the whole mixture on your lap and spend the rest of the afternoon greeting clients as a mess of brown stains and bandages.

If you like to dunk, you'll be glad to know that, after a two-month study employing high-tech equipment, Dr Len Fisher and his team of researchers at the University of Bristol discovered the mathematical formula that determines the ideal dunking technique and time to maximize the biscuit-to-mush ratio.

Biscuits are starch held together by sugar. When a hot liquid enters its pores, the sugar melts and the structure becomes unstable. As this occurs, ten times more flavour is released than when you eat a dry biscuit. That's why we do it. But, as Fisher told the BBC, 'You have got a race between the dissolving of the sugar and your biscuit falling apart and a swelling of the starch grains so that they stick together, giving you a biscuit which is purely starch but rather softer than what you started with.'

To determine the perfect dunking time, Fisher coated a digestive in 24-carat gold so he could scan it with an electron microscope and reveal its internal structure. Then he wet the biscuit on one side and filmed the progress of the tea as it seeped in. Finally, he used an Instron machine to measure how much the biscuit was affected by the moisture.

Using a mathematical formula – the average pore diameter in a biscuit is equal to four times the viscosity of the hot liquid, multiplied by the height the liquid rises squared, divided by the surface tension of the beverage, multiplied by the length of time the biscuit is dunked – Fisher determined that most digestive-style biscuits should remain in a hot drink for 3.5 seconds. He also revealed the perfect dunking technique. Using a wide-brimmed mug, the biscuit should be dipped at a shallow angle and, after the dunk, it should be rotated 180 degrees so the dry side supports the wet side. Of course, the timing will be slightly different with softer biscuits. Fortunately, Fisher plans to publish a table that defines the ideal dunking times for various types of biscuit.

Music over 90 decibels may trigger the sacculus to send a jolt to the hypothalamus.

Hypothalamus, which controls desire for food and sex

Sacculus

Eardrum

Inner ear

BOOMING CAR STEREOS

See also *Off-key Singing*.

B oom, Boom, Boom, Boom . . . I'm trying to sleep here! Boom, BOOM, BOOM, Boom . . . Your teenage son's car has been fitted with supermega-mondo-killer-ultimate-platinum bass speakers. When they're cranked up – which they always are – the car shakes, glass breaks, dogs howl and small animals run for cover. Your son just bops his multiple-pierced head in appreciation.

Boom-cars are primarily a male obsession. The most devoted enthusiasts of booming music spend thousands of pounds on their audio systems and enter their souped-up cars in competitions. The loudest car stereo competition winners of the past few years have blasted in at 155 to 160 decibels, more than twice as loud as a jet taking off and definitely loud enough to cause permanent hearing damage. It takes only about 115 decibels to do that. Emergency sirens, at 120 decibels, don't stand a chance against the loudest boomers.

Robert Franner, editor of the Toronto-based audio trade publication *Marketnews*, once compared sound level competitions to 'comparing genitals'. He went on: 'It's overkill for people with naturally occurring high levels of testosterone.'

Franner may not be too far off. Young males use their booming cars to draw attention, mark territory and to draw the attention of females. Recent research shows that a boom-car is something of a sexual stimulant on wheels. A 2000 study by Manchester University found that loud music stimulates a part of the ear that is connected to the brain's pleasure centre.

The sacculus, a tiny organ in the inner ear, is part of the system that controls the sense of balance. It does not appear to serve any function in hearing, but it does send messages to the hypothalamus, which controls the human appetite for food and sex. The sacculus is sensitive to sounds over 90 decibels, which may send a kind of pleasure jolt to the brain.

'The distribution of frequencies that are typical in rock concerts and at dance clubs almost seem designed to stimulate the sacculus,' Neil Todd, who led the research team, told *New Scientist*. 'They are absolutely smack bang in this range of sensitivity.'

The pleasure may be addictive. Researchers at Northeastern University in Boston, Massachusetts, identified what they call Maladaptive Music Listening. People who suffer from MML can't seem to stop listening to loud music even when it is literally deafening. Deprived of a daily loud music blast, the subjects suffered withdrawal symptoms including depression, moodiness and lethargy. Music over 90 decibels may trigger the sacculus to send a jolt to the hypothalamus.

BUFFERING

See also *Too Many Streaming Services*.

You have invited your best friends over to your house to binge-watch the new season of *House of Cards*. The popcorn is popped, you've navigated to your streaming service and you push play. After five minutes the picture freezes, the dreaded loading thermometer appears on the screen, and you wait, and wait . . .

We love to stream. Six billion hours of YouTube are streamed every month. That is billion with a B. Netflix subscribers alone streamed 42.5 billion hours of programming in 2015. Being able to stream just about any programme at any time is one of the joys of the modern age. Having the programmes freeze and stop is one of the pains.

When a video streams, it's playing as it downloads rather than being downloaded completely before playing on a local machine. Buffering is when a certain amount of data is downloaded before playback begins so that you do not watch faster than you download. When your streaming gets ahead of the downloading, you experience an interrupt. The larger the size of your buffer, the less likely the playback is to be interrupted. When it works well, buffering is a good thing. But we usually encounter the word 'buffering' when things are not working well.

A 2016 study sponsored by the mobile telephone company Ericsson monitored people's brain activity, eye movements and pulse while doing different everyday smartphone tasks. What did they learn? Slow-loading web pages, buffering and interrupted videos stress us out. Users' heart rates increased an average of 38 per cent when content was delayed. Their stress level was 'similar to that of watching a horror movie or solving a mathematical problem and greater than waiting in a checkout line at the grocery store,' the report said.

If you're having trouble getting that cat video on YouTube to play properly, there are a few things you can try. First off, make sure you're not running a bunch of programs or apps on your device. Streaming a video takes memory. So closing those programs can help. If the service allows it, pressing pause and letting more of the video download before playback can help. Or start again from the beginning. With any luck, by the time you get back to the part of the film where it got hung up, more data will have downloaded and you can proceed normally. If none of this works, you might try logging on at another time. According to the Federal Communications Commission (FCC) in the United States, most streaming occurs between 7 and 11pm. When servers get more demand than they can handle, everything slows down. Your experience will probably be better at 3am. Of course, getting up in the middle of the night to watch a movie is also a little bit annoying.

Incidentally, there are two kinds of symbols that show up when digital content is downloading. The throbber is the spinner that lets you know something is happening, but not how long it will take. Then there's a progress bar that appears to tell you how much progress you've made, but actually lies to you. Most of the time, says *Popular Mechanics*, a progress bar that says 50 per cent complete could be half done, or it could be just starting. Estimating how long it will take to download or install something is complicated. Most app developers don't really try. They use an off-the-rack code to give a broad ballpark estimate. They are, however, trying to come up with ways to make it seem faster.

Chris Harrison, a PhD candidate at Carnegie Mellon University, tested a variety of animations to come up with the most pleasing tracker. It speeds up as it progresses, and contains a ripple animation that moves backwards. This gives the impression that things are moving along, even when they are really not.

BUREAUCRACY, OR 'IT SAYS SO ON MY SCREEN'

See also *Dead Pens*.

A s a general rule, you are not going to be whistling 'Zip-A-Dee-Doo-Dah' in any situation that requires you to use a number to identify yourself. According to one estimate, Americans spend a collective 6.1 billion hours a year filling out tax forms. Despite rosy predictions of the paperless office, the amount of paper we churn out continues to grow. Coopers & Lybrand estimate that there are over 4 trillion paper documents in the United States alone. But it is not drowning in paperwork that gets our goat; it is encountering impersonal, unyielding systems that make us feel like cogs in the wheel. The notion behind bureaucratic structures is highly democratic. It assumes that most people and situations follow similar patterns and that, if rules are put in place to guide behaviour, everything should run smoothly. The problem is, bureaucracy doesn't respond at all well to novel situations and it is not known for making compassionate, or even logical, exceptions to its rules.

We tend to think of a 'bureaucrat' as a sort of job position. In truth, bureaucracy is a state of mind. A bureaucrat is a person with a personality and value system that says the letter of the law is meant to be followed regardless of logic or underlying circumstances – it says so right here on my screen. It is true that they are often found in government offices, but they can also be found at airports, post offices and gyms. James H Boren, author of *Fuzzify*, coined the collective noun 'a mumble of bureaucrats' for them. As organizations become bigger and more impersonal, 'rules are rules' systems and administrators become more and more prevalent. A bureaucrat is someone who does not feel he or she has the authority to make exceptions, and who likes not having that responsibility.

The people who are most frustrated by this mentality are those who can't get beyond the naive belief that the underlying reality is supposed to matter. Go ahead. Keep believing that. It will cause you nothing but grief. Go write a rock song about 'The Man' if you must, but your visa application will be denied if you send it to the address in the current printed instructions and not the one listed in the updated booklet that the Foreign Office plans to print next year. (Seriously, don't get me started on this one!)

The best you can do is try to figure out how to use the letter of the law to your own advantage. As Gordon MacKenzie put it in his excellent little book *Orbiting the Giant Hairball* (the hairball being the bureaucratic office environment), 'anytime a bureaucrat (i.e., a custodian of a system) stands between you and something you need or want, your challenge is to help that bureaucrat discover a means, harmonious with the system, to meet your need.'

The biggest mistake you can make in trying to put an end to a bureaucratic stand-off is to ask a bureaucrat to bend the rules. She wants to keep everything humming along properly. Rules keep us equal. You will not change such a person's core belief in the beauty and equality of the system. If you want to get what you want, you will have to be a little creative, and to think like a bureaucrat yourself. Rule books are thick, dense and full of regulations that you can use in your favour.

Follow the example of Helen O'Neil. In the early 1980s the artist found a home with a charming 125-year-old barn on a large plot in Rochester Hills, Michigan, an area that was quickly changing in character from rural to suburban. She thought the barn would make a wonderfully romantic pottery shed and workshop. After doing it up, she put her works on display and started teaching pottery classes.

That's when the city council got involved. They ordered her to remove the 'O'Neil Pottery' sign outside her property because a town ordinance prohibited commercial signs. Helen was undeterred. She had her name legally changed to 'O'Neil-Pottery'. There was no law against putting your own name on your postbox or fence, was there?

CAR ALARMS ▶ CRACKING KNUCKLES

C

CAR ALARMS

See also *Booming Car Stereos, Noise.*

I t's 3am. You are in the middle of that dream where you are flying over your childhood home when EEAAAEEEEAAAAEEEE . . . It's your neighbour's car alarm. Do you a) rush outside to foil the robbery in progress, b) immediately call the police, or c) put your pillow over your head and mutter '@#$% car alarms'.

Chances are, you picked c. Separate studies in both New York City and Los Angeles found that 95 per cent of alarms are false. Smaller cities have had similar results. Everyone knows it, so no one pays much attention to the shrill sound – at least not as a warning. It is still very effective as a sleep deterrent.

'You have a car thief attacking your car. You're going to run out, and you're going to do . . . what?' vehicle security expert Reg Phillips asked a reporter for the *Atlantic*.

Annoyed woman

EEEAAAEEEAAAA

Bump by handbag

DLX6

New York City councillors say there is no evidence that audible alarms deter car theft. Experienced thieves can make off with your vehicle in a matter of seconds. One Los Angeles policeman confessed that he put a car alarm only one step higher on his priority scale than 'a car blocking a driveway'.

Apparently, in urban areas there are so many alarm-equipped vehicles, and they go off so often, no one recognizes the sound of his own car being invaded. To make it easier, alarm makers have made it possible for consumers to choose exactly what ear-splitting combination of tones they want. The wail is not only loud, it is designed to grate. It is high-pitched with repeating multi-tones. A typical siren has six tones so it can be customized . . . and infuriating.

A 2003 report estimated that New York's car alarms alone lead to about $400 to $500 million per year in 'public-health costs, lost productivity, decreased property value, and diminished quality of life'. Of course, this study was conducted by Transportation Alternatives, an organization that would like to see the city's cars replaced with bicycles.

To work out just how annoying car alarms were, they used the equation $(V \times APF) \times (N \times NDI) = 1$ minute's worth of car alarm damage to the average New York City resident. V is the value of a New York minute, APF is the Aggravation Persistence Factor, N is noise and NDI is the Noise Depreciation Index.

Despite their questionable effectiveness, and the annoyance factor, audible car alarms remain the most common form of theft deterrent for vehicles. This is true in spite of the fact that there are low tech and quiet alternatives such as a steering wheel lock that are much more effective. There are now a number of high-tech solutions as well, including car tracking systems that can lead police straight to a stolen vehicle and 'immobilizers' that shut off the ignition unless you have a key with the right computer chip embedded in it. Of course, thieves are a crafty lot, and already they have found ways to hack highly computerized security systems. It seems having to outwit criminals is the real aggravation.

CAR PARK BATTLES, OR 'GET OUT OF MY SPACE!'

f cities are 'urban jungles', car parks are our territorial battlegrounds. As soon as we see an open spot, we claim it in the name of our SUV. Driving gets all of the glory but parking is really what cars do. Our cars are parked on average 95 per cent of the time. That means we need a lot of spaces, which leads to competition and anxiety. (Like when you're coming up to what appears to be an empty space in an almost-full car park only to discover there's a Smart Car wedged way up in the front so you can't see it until you're about to pull in.) Once we've bagged a prime spot, we're willing to fight anyone who tries to prevent us from possessing it. A survey by Bernice Kanner, author of *Are You Normal?*, asked Americans what they would do if they arrived at a parking spot at the same time as another driver. Almost two-thirds said they would fight for it. Northeastern drivers were the most stubborn; 79 per cent said they'd rather fight than give up the space, compared to 40 per cent of Midwesterners. If your car is already comfortably entrenched in a space, the situation doesn't change much.

Pennsylvania State University researchers Barry Ruback and Daniel Juieng conducted a study of more than 400 drivers at an Atlanta-area mall car park. They reported their findings in the article 'Territorial Defense in Parking Lots: Retaliation against Waiting Drivers' in the *Journal of Applied Social Psychology*. They discovered departing drivers took 7 seconds longer to get out of a spot when someone was waiting for it than when no one was there. If the waiting driver beeped, the departing driver became even slower. The wait jumped from 32.2 seconds (with no one waiting) to 43 seconds. There are a few things you can do to reduce your parking stress. People who study such things for a living say that you're better off taking the first place you see rather than driving around looking for a prime location. It turns out that parking hunters not only waste time driving in circles, they end up on average no closer to the door. Women, incidentally, are more likely to drive around in search of the closest spot than men. Women have more parking anxiety and take more time pulling into a spot, but at least one study suggests that the world is better for it. British women, at least, are better parkers. In a study by the firm NCP, which employed a team of researchers to observe 2,500 drivers across its 700 car parks, women did a better job of parking in the middle of their spots. Men, however, were more likely to say they were excellent parkers.

CAR SEAT CONFUSION

See also *Some Assembly Required.*

You are an intelligent person with an advanced degree. Why does putting the child's car seat in make you want to tear your hair out? And how can you be sure you've done it right?

It's not just you. The editors of *Consumer Reports*, who test hundreds of child car seats in different vehicles each year, are equally challenged. 'Even with our combined experience, we routinely find ourselves challenged by complicated car-seat instruction manuals and installations. If we're having such a hard time, we wonder, how would a parent who doesn't have much experience figure this all out?'

The answer, sad to say, is that they don't.

In a recent study in the United States by the National Highway Traffic Safety Administration, new parents asked to install an infant seat did the job incorrectly between 95 and 100 per cent of the time . . . 95 and 100 per cent! More experienced users fared a bit better, but even they put the seats in too loosely about half of the time. Most of them believed they had done it correctly.

You have probably heard the advice 'When all else fails read the instructions'. In this case, you will have to read two sets of instructions, those of the manufacturer of the car seat and your car's owner's manual. While most parents know enough to read the first, they don't realize that there may be pertinent information in the second manual as well.

The thing you're most likely to get wrong is leaving the seat too loose. When installed correctly, a child seat should move no more than an inch in any direction. There are two systems for attaching a car seat – the seatbelt system and what is known as the ISOFIX system in Europe, or LATCH in the USA. It was designed to make seat installation easier.

Either system is safe if done correctly. If you do use the ISOFIX or LATCH system, do not use a seatbelt installation too. This is not a case where more is better.

It is also possible that your car's design is not helping you. A recent

C

US survey by the Insurance Institute for Highway Safety found that only about 20 per cent of the popular vehicles they studied had hardware that made it easy to access the anchors that hold safety seats in place.

The second most common thing parents get wrong is putting the rear-facing infant car seat at the wrong angle. The seat should be set with a 30- to 45-degree angle in order to keep the baby's head back and prevent it from falling forwards and obstructing the airway. If the seat does not have an adjustment knob, you may need to put a rolled towel underneath to get it right.

As much as you would like to look back and see your child's smiling face, do not switch to a forward-facing car seat until your child is two years old or the maximum height and weight allowed by the car seat manufacturer. A child should stay in a forward-facing car seat with a harness until he or she has reached the maximum weight – generally 15 to 36kg (33 to 80lb). A booster seat should be used after that until the child reaches the age of 12 or the height of 135cm (4ft 5in). After that, it is safe to use just a seat belt.

Make sure your child is strapped in tight. If you can still pinch the fabric of the harness straps between your fingers, it is too lose. The straps should not have any slack.

If you are not sure you've done everything right – or even if you think you have – you can visit a car seat inspection event for help from the experts. Search online for Child Seat Safety to find an expert in your area.

CATS SHREDDING FURNITURE

See also *Dogs Sniffing Your Privates, Fleas*.

Some people have nice furniture – people without cats. You, on the other hand, have sofas with vertical rips that bleed stuffing. Sure, Fluffy is cute when she purrs, but when she scratches your furniture to bits you want to take about eight of her nine lives.

One of the reasons a cat scratches is to peel the old sheaths off its nails. Scratching also seems to be a form of exercise. Yet the most important reason Fluffy claws away may be to mark her territory.

The domestic cat has not strayed far from its wild origins. She may seem like a cuddly household pet, but in her mind she is a big game hunter. In the wild a cat has a large territory, depending on its gender. Males patrol about 60 hectares (about 150 acres) and females about 6 hectares (15 acres). They are looking for food and mates and trying to keep other cats away from their food and mates. Since you give your cat all the food she needs, and she has been spayed, she shouldn't need to obsessively mark and guard her personal space – but she still does.

T S Eliot got it right when he wrote a poem about the cat that was 'always on the wrong side of the door'. You let Fluffy out, two minutes later she is scratching at the window demanding to be let in. Two minutes after that, she is meowing at the door, ready to go back out.

'Cats are very territorial animals,' says Betsy Lipscomb, president of Cats International. 'They have to investigate every square inch of their territory. They have to patrol it on a regular basis. Wherever their little paws have walked, that's now their territory. If the door is closed – they've been in that room before, they want to go in there and check it out on a regular basis. That's why they hate closed doors. It interferes with their job. They have a great duty.'

Your cat requires the assistance of your opposable thumbs to get to the other side of that door, and she would rather have your begrudging help than wait around to check if there is a hideous beast lurking in part of her territory.

'Felines in general are dominant creatures,' says California veterinarian Petra Drake. 'Big cats such as lions and tigers are all basically at the top of the food chain with very little real threat of predator action against them. With this level of domination, big cats are able to exert tremendous control over their environment. Their movement in and around their territory is at will and constrained only by whim. Take this genetic endowment of environmental control and place it into a ten pound feline then stick in it a domestic setting. You get a wonderfully entitled creature who refuses to be constrained by a simple mechanical door handle.' The scratching is part of this primitive impulse. It not only leaves a visible mark, it also leaves an odour for other cats to smell. The scent is secreted through glands in the cat's paws. This is why declawed cats keep trying to scratch. They are still able to spread their scent.

In order to change Fluffy's habits, you will have to doctor your furniture for a little while. You can try putting double-sided masking tape on the corners of the furniture or covering the entire piece of furniture with a sheet. Where you put the scratching post is also important. Put it near the thing the cat most loves to destroy.

Scratching helps to peel old layers of nails off claws.

Fluffy

Your favourite sofa

C

Gum sticking to shoe by Van der Waals force

Gum on street

Your shoe

CHEWING GUM POLLUTION, OR GUMFITTI

Y ou are on your first date with the cute red-haired guy you've had your eye on for weeks. He takes you to a pavement café. You're both smiling and chatting pleasantly until you cross your legs and the knee of your silk trousers gets stuck to the table by an oversize wad of dirty chewing gum that someone parked underneath. Not only are your trousers ruined, but the expletives coming out of your once sweet, feminine mouth have ruined any chance that you will ever have children with freckles.

Americans didn't invent chewing gum. According to the *Independent*, a university researcher named Elizabeth Aveling concluded from tooth marks in prehistoric tar that children have been chewing gum in northern Europe since about 7000 BCE. Americans have certainly taken to the habit, though. Modern chewing gum is made out of 40 to 50 compounds including pine tree resin, petroleum products, wax and synthetic latexes. You're basically chewing a stickier version of the stuff they use to cover golf balls. It doesn't go away, so when the sugar and flavourings have disappeared, the gooey lump has to go somewhere.

It's surprising we're not all stuck in place from the gum on the soles of our shoes. If you take a good look at a city pavement you will see black spots. That's ground-in, dirt-encrusted, already-been-chewed gum. It's expensive and time-consuming to remove. You can freeze it with Freon and scrape it up; smear it with citric acid-based chemicals and wait for it to dissolve; try to melt it away with hot water and chemicals, or 'power-wash' it with pressures of 2,000 pounds per square inch. Sometimes this process damages the pavement without getting up the gum.

Gum is so sticky it almost defies the laws of physics. It is, in fact, about 10,000 times stickier than theoretical models say it should be. Chewing gum, like adhesive tape, owes its stickiness primarily to the Van der Waals force, an electric force that acts between uncharged molecules. When experimenters measured the amount of energy needed to pull a metallic probe off a sticky surface, however, they discovered it took more force than would be needed to overcome Van der Waals.

A pair of French researchers set out to find out why. Cyprien Gay, a physicist with the Centre national de la recherche scientifique in Paris, and Ludwik Leibler of Elf Atochem, a French chemical company, devised a model that explains chewing gum's sticky behaviour. When your shoe comes down on a piece of chewing gum, the boundaries of the rubber sole and the gum's surface come together. Air is trapped between them. As you pull your shoe away, the bubbles are stretched. They behave like tiny suction cups, which makes it harder to pull the gum away from the shoe and the shoe away from the gum.

The good news for public health is that Americans, at least, are chewing less of the stuff than in days gone by. Gum sales in the United States have been declining since 2010. It all depends on where you live. Just as some are dropping the habit, chewers in China, Russia and Mexico are taking up the sticky slack. Between 2009 and 2014 the global gum market grew 20 per cent to about £19.4 billion. Let's hope our neighbours are better at finding rubbish bins.

CHILDREN'S STORIES OVER AND OVER AND . . .

How many times does your child want you to read him *The Gruffalo*? About fifty-seven more times than you want to read it. Your daughter, meanwhile, wants to see *Frozen*, for the ninety-sixth time. Parents have been known to 'lose' books, to suddenly 'forget' how to read or speak English, or to 'accidentally' reverse over the DVD with the car . . . five times in a row.

Listening to the same story over and over is part of the process that builds the neural pathways that form memory. As Peter Ornstein, Professor of Psychology at the University of North Carolina at Chapel Hill, explained in *Parenting* magazine, 'The narrative form is the scaffolding and support for remembering.' The first time a child hears a story or sees a film, he starts to connect the elements of the story to other experiences. Thus he creates new neural connections, but the connections are tenuous. To build stronger connections, he must reinforce it by repeating the experience.

'The child gets to connect these experiences with other kinds of experiences they've had by watching it over again,' says Mary Mindess, a long-time professor of early-childhood education at Lesley University in Cambridge, Massachusetts. 'It makes those neural connections stronger and therefore able to branch out and make other kinds of connections. The story for them becomes more powerful each time they hear it.'

There is also an emotional component. Favourite stories evoke strong emotions, joy, excitement and catharsis. Children want to feel those emotions again, and they know they can do so by hearing the same story. 'Young children like to have a sense of power,' says Mindess. 'The more they can hear the story, the more they can act the part of the story that gives them an additional sense of what they want to try to accomplish. Adults have more avenues for getting the repetition of the same emotional experience than the child has. The child doesn't have as many avenues to seek out, so he likes the repeat of things because he's pretty sure he knows what's going to happen.'

The bad news is, there's not really anything you can do to rush through this stage of development. So buckle down and read *The Cat in the Hat* one more time. The good news is, they do eventually grow out of it, and one day the book you couldn't stand to pick up will fill you with affectionate nostalgia.

Child, 3–8 years old

Tattered children's book

Father

C

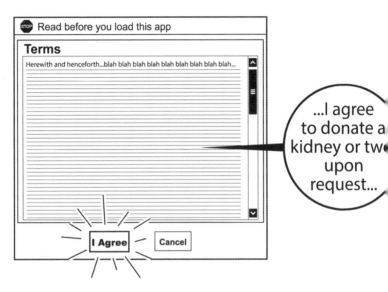

CLICKWRAP:
BY READING THIS YOU AGREE
TO THE TERMS OF SERVICE

See also *Buffering, Computer Viruses, Pop-up Ads, Trolls, Unfriended.*

You are about to install that cool new app, sign up for an online subscription or buy a book from an online retailer. Before you complete the transaction a screen appears in front of you with a scroll bar asking you to agree to the terms of service to continue. You read it right? Of course you don't. Nobody reads it.

We generally don't view these click-through documents as important information, but rather as an irritating obstacle to getting to the content or service we want. How do we know no one reads those agreements? In 2016 a pair of researchers from two different universities did a little test. They created a fictional social networking site called NameDrop and had subjects sign up. Given the option, 74 per cent of the study participants skipped over the privacy policy and opted for a 'quick join'. It took them, on average, 73 seconds to scan the privacy policy and 51 seconds to scan the terms of service. Based on average adult reading speed, if they had actually read and comprehended the material, it should have taken half an hour to get through the privacy policy and 16 minutes for the terms of service.

Lest you think the researchers happened to have assembled a group of speed-readers, there is further evidence that they skipped through the terms of service without reading it. The privacy policy said that anything posted on the network could be shared with the NSA 'and other security agencies in the United States and abroad'. It also said that your data could be shared with any third parties, and as a result noted that membership in the site could 'impact eligibility in . . . employment, financial service, university entrance, international travel, the criminal justice system, etc.' And, in spite of the fact that the terms of service required the payment of 'a first-born child' to access the service, fully 98 per cent agreed. In a similar experiment in the UK in 2014, users were also willing to sign away their first-borns. A 2010 experiment conducted by a British retail site had users giving up their 'immortal souls'.

Yet the courts have held that so-called clickwrap is a legally binding agreement. You may not have read it, but you could have, and it is up to you to know what you are agreeing to. So clearly it behoves us to read the digital fine print. Here's the thing, we couldn't even if we wanted to because we have lives. A team of researchers at Carnegie Melon University calculated that to read all of the various legal texts we encounter in a year would take 25 days. If you were to sit down and read them in eight-hour blocks, you would need 76 work days to complete the task. Collectively, that is 53.8 billion hours a year just reading terms of service and privacy policies. The researchers estimated that if we actually did this, the value of the lost productivity would be $781 billion – that's more than the GDP of Florida.

C

Even if we had that kind of time, a lot of us could not make sense of the documents anyway. Researchers at Georgia Tech surveyed the terms of service agreements of the top 30 social media and fan sites and found that you need to possess the average reading level of a graduate to understand them. That means 60 per cent of the population do not have the education level required to make an informed decision before clicking.

The fact that we don't know what rights we've signed away leads to some paranoid meme sharing. There are periodic online waves of people posting a legal-sounding status saying that the user does not grant Facebook the right to claim copyright over the birthday pictures and status updates you post. Various versions have circulated over the years. Don't share these things. They usually get the facts wrong, and, anyway, you can't unilaterally change the contractual terms you agreed to when you signed up to a service by posting something on your wall. The periodic outbreaks of these viral messages only goes to show that we would rather click share than search out the actual privacy policy and read what's in it.

Is it fair that companies can create and legally enforce contracts that they know are not read? Probably not but the courts have spoken, and that is the way it is. There is a little bit of help out there. 'Useable Privacy', a website launched jointly by Carnegie Mellon University and Fordham Law School, analyses the privacy policies of various services and translates them into normal English so you don't have to. You can try it out at explore.usableprivacy.org.

CLINGFILM THAT STICKS TO ITSELF

See also *Dead Pens*.

You spent 15 minutes baking a tray of cookies to take to your book group coffee morning. You put them on a plate and get out the box of clingfilm. You spend the next 20 minutes trying to get the film to unroll and stick to anything but itself. Clingfilm is known as clingfilm for good reason. It is designed to cling. The trick is to get it to stick to containers and not to your fingers.

Clingfilm is made of a resin called polyvinyl chloride. The resin was discovered in 1933 by Ralph Wiley, an employee at Dow Chemical. Wiley had the low-level task of scrubbing the glassware in the lab and he discovered a vial coated with a substance that would not come off. The Dow researchers took an interest in the goop and made it into a spray film to use on fighter planes to guard against corrosion from sea salt. After the Second World War the company looked for ways to market it to home consumers and food wrap was born.

The wrap's clinginess comes from its electrical charge, which combines with the charge of the container. If a glass has a negative charge on its surface, for example, clingfilm with a positive charge will stick well. The reason film sticks so well in some cases and so poorly in others has to do with differences in electrical fields of various containers and their materials.

To win the battle with clingfilm, store your roll in the fridge or freezer. When it is cold it is easier to handle and less likely to stick to itself. It will quickly warm up and return to clinging when you drape it over your delicious cookies.

C

COFFEE SPILLS

See also *Biscuit Mush*.

You make a fresh cup of coffee in the office kitchen. You blow on it, take a quick sip and start to walk back to your desk. How long will it take for you to slosh it all over your new blouse? About eight steps, say scientists.

Coffee slosh is a simple case a fluid dynamics, and yes, University of California at Santa Barbara scientists have studied it using cameras and sensors on mugs. They calculated the natural frequency at which coffee sloshes back and forth when held in typical mugs of different sizes. They learned that coffee's frequency is the same as a person's natural gait. This causes the liquid to oscillate. Somewhere between the seventh and tenth step the coffee will slosh over the rim.

Some of your natural instincts make things worse. Coffee drinkers often try to walk quickly with their cups to get back to their desks before they spill, but the faster you move the closer your gait comes to the natural sloshing frequency of the coffee. You are better off walking slowly. Accelerate gradually. If you bolt away you will create a big wave. You also want to avoid changing your pace. This results in wider oscillations or, to put it in layman's terms, more sloshing.

Their scientific solution is to walk more slowly and to fill your mug less. Here is the formula: the gap between the top of the coffee and the rim should be at least one-eighth of the mug's diameter. If that doesn't work, there are always travel mugs with lids.

Of course, you don't need to be moving to make a mess with your caffeine fix. Is your desk covered in brown rings? You will be pleased to know that a number of years ago Robert D Deegan, Sidney R Nagel and their co-workers at the James Franck Institute of the University of Chicago answered the age-old question, 'Why does spilled coffee dry in an ugly ring?' The team published their findings in the journal *Nature* in an article called 'Capillary Flow as the Cause of Ring Stains from Dried Liquid Drops.'

The researchers had puzzled over coffee rings for some time. They theorized that perhaps tiny electrical charges around the ring trapped the dissolved coffee particles, but when they did the maths they found that it would take hours for the particles to form that pattern. Coffee dries much more quickly than that. They experimented by drying the drop upside down and putting it on clean silicone. They still got rings. The chemical composition of coffee could not be to blame because other liquids – tea, wine, milk – leave circles of their own.

Then one day a graduate student, Olgica Bakajin, did an experiment of his own. Before a drop dried, he covered most of it. The part of the drop that had not been exposed to air did not form a ring. They theorized that the edge of the drop gets stuck because of irregularities in the table's surface, and surface tension keeps it in a drop shape. Liquid evaporates from the edge of the drop, where it thins and coffee from the centre of the drop rolls outwards to replace it. By the time it evaporates completely, almost all of the coffee has flowed to the edge.

To test their theory, the researchers suspended polystyrene spheres in a water droplet on a microscope slide. They videotaped the solution as it dispersed and, as predicted, it formed a ring. Next time someone comments on your coffee-stained worktops, tell them you're just doing a science experiment.

COMMON COLD

See also *Coughing in the Theatre*.

I t's not a big deal, it's just a cold. Not even worth calling in sick. You will just sit at your desk and hold your nose with a Kleenex while you fight the headaches, fever and chills.

Different people have different reactions to colds. Most people, 95 per cent, who are exposed to the rhino viruses that cause a cold do become infected, but only 75 per cent get any symptoms.

People who are lucky enough not to feel sick fight off the infection just as well as you do with your runny nose and endless sneezing. Lucky them. Your dog and cat are immune to colds as well. The cold is only common to humans, chimpanzees and higher primates. Feel better?

Cold viruses can live for a short time on a surface, say, someone's hand. Shake hands with that person and you get the cold virus on your hand then you rub your nose and voilà, the process begins. As little as a single particle of the virus is all that is needed to mount an infection. You breathe in and the virus, which contains strands of genetic coding coated in protein, is transported to the back of the nose by the nose itself. There it attaches itself to a receptor, which transports it into a cell in the respiratory track. Once it's in its cell, the virus can reproduce. More and more virus particles are created until finally the host cell bursts and the doses of virus infects new cells and the process starts anew. The whole thing takes about eight to twelve hours.

It takes about ten hours for the body to start mounting its defence. The inflammatory mediators histamine, kinins, interleukins and prostaglandins cause your blood vessels to dilate so they can transport water and other materials needed to create extra mucus. Mucus is your nose's defence to just about any irritant. Unfortunately, the cold virus it is trying to flush out is hidden away safe within the walls of a nasal cell most of the time. However, the sneezing, coughing and nose blowing do have one effect – they help to spread colds to other people. There is some truth to the old wives' tale about chicken soup.

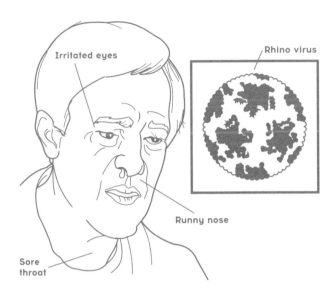

Irritated eyes

Rhino virus

Runny nose

Sore
throat

If you're all stuffed up, the soup will loosen things up a bit; that is the conclusion of three clinicians who published the article 'Effects of Drinking Hot Water, Cold Water and Chicken Soup on Nasal Mucus Velocity and Nasal Airflow Resistance' in the medical journal *Chest*. Hot chicken soup increased mucus velocity from 6.9 to 9.2 millimetres per minute, a result that is 'statistically significant' compared to cold water and hot water. The faster the mucus velocity, that is, how much mucus is expelled from the body, the faster the infected cells are expelled from the body (and spread to other people). The researchers concluded, 'hot chicken soup, either through the aroma sensed at the posterior nares or through a mechanism related to taste, appears to possess an additional substance for increasing nasal mucus velocity'. Go and tell your mum she was right.

COMPUTER VIRUSES

See also *Buffering, Keyboard Crud, Trolls.*

Your computer is behaving strangely. Very strangely. You delete a file, and it seems to pop up again in another directory. Delete it again, it reappears somewhere else. There were a few documents in one file that you can't find anywhere now. What's going on? Suddenly a message pops up on your screen, 'Super Hacker Strikes Again'. You forgot to update your virus scanner's database, didn't you?

Being attacked by a computer virus is like being robbed or having your windows broken by a vandal. You feel violated, even if the virus did little damage. If it deletes files, rewords important documents or causes your computer to crash, it can have far-reaching consequences.

According to Symantec, in 2015 nearly 317 million computer viruses were unleashed on the unsuspecting world. That is almost a million a day.

In the bad old days of early computing, computer viruses were often created by teenaged hackers who competed for bragging rights on how far their creations were able to spread in the wild. These were malicious pranks that relied on human nature to get people to download and execute email attachments and games with Trojan horses inside them. If you're nostalgic for those simpler times, you can visit the Malware Museum's virus collection, which simulates (without the annoyance of actually going viral) some of the invasive coding from DOS days (archive.org/details/malwaremuseum&tab=collection).

The hackers of old wanted to take credit for their work, and their viruses were accordingly flashy. (One that affected this author replaced random words in Word documents with 'wazoo'.)

These days you're more likely to get a virus from a link on a social media site than from downloading an email attachment. The people who program viruses also have more sinister motives than their ancestors. A lot of them are trying to install keyloggers and other programs that steal your personal information, or they want to run in the background and use your computer as part of a network of spam marketing machines. An increasing problem is cyber ransom, where a tech-savvy blackmailer steals important data like photos or the only copy of your dissertation and then demands a ransom to unencrypt or return it.

These days, viruses often pass unnoticed. If your computer is suddenly running slowly or your hard drive is always spinning no matter how few resources you think you're using, there may be something going on in the background and it is time to run a virus/malware scanner.

I could end this entry with all of the standard advice about safe computing, keeping your antivirus definitions up to date, downloading the latest security updates on all your software, not downloading or clicking on content from strangers or doing regular backups, but you have heard it all before. It is a constant battle between the forces creating malicious software and those creating the defences against them. It is an annoyance that is not going to go away soon.

COUGHING IN THE THEATRE

See also *Rustling Sweet Wrappers*.

Y ou are simply trying to hear the orchestra. Hack, hack, cough, cough, wheeze. Violins. Hacking. Cellos, throat clearing. Brass and phlegm. It bothers the performers, too. At a concert by the Carnegie Hall Jazz Band in Minneapolis, the musical director, Jon Faddis, stopped and chided audience members for their coughing.

In 1975 the Dallas Opera performed *Tristan und Isolde* and Jon Vickers, as Tristan, was lying flat on the stage while another singer was trying valiantly to be heard over a virtual cough concert. Vickers had enough and shouted: 'Shut up with your damn coughing!' Opera singer Marilyn Horne once observed that the worst coughing occurs in cities with sunny climates, such as Dallas and Miami. In cities with long spells of damp, cold weather, the audiences are quiet.

Psychology may be as much to blame as itchy throats. During dramatic moments, when the audience is rapt, coughing subsides. When the crowd becomes restless, the coughing resumes. Sometimes though, you just get that tickle in your throat and there's not much you can do.

Many theatres have taken to providing free cough drops, but then there is the problem of unwrapping them. There is a trick to coughing in a theatre without making noise. According to Florence B Blager, chief of the speech pathology and audiology service at the National Jewish Center for Immunology and Respiratory Medicine in Denver, you should not stifle the cough, but let the air explode outwards. When you feel the cough begin, blow air through tightly pursed lips. This gets rid of the air a cough would expel without going through the vocal chords. We haven't tried this ourselves, but Blager insists it can be done with a little practice. If you fail to develop this skill, Judith Martin, author of the syndicated 'Miss Manners' column, says that if you cough more than three times, you should leave the theatre.

CRACKING KNUCKLES

I f you have a friend or co-worker who habitually cracks his knuckles, you would probably like me to tell you that it causes disease, ozone depletion and nuclear war. Anything that would scare the person enough to make him STOP. Sorry, I can't help you.

What happens inside the hands of a person who cracks his knuckles may be damaging to your nerves, but it is not particularly damaging to the knuckle cracker. Each joint is surrounded by fluid that fills the gap between the bones. Ligaments surround the whole thing and hold the joints together. When you put pressure on your finger, the pressure drops between the bones and the ligament is pulled in by the small vacuum. At the same time, gas is forced out of the knuckle forming a bubble. The bubble takes up the space between the bones, and the ligament snaps back into its original position with the familiar popping sound.

Contrary to popular belief, habitual knuckle cracking does not cause arthritis or deformed joints. As Dr Dave Hnida told *CBS This Morning*, 'Probably the biggest problem with cracking your knuckles is that it annoys everybody else that you're around.' If you are looking for an honest reason to dissuade that knuckle-cracking colleague, however, one study of people who had regularly cracked their knuckles over a period of 35 years showed they had slightly swollen joints and a weaker grip than non-knuckle crackers. If you're the one in the habit of cracking your knuckles, doctors recommend doing something else like squeezing on a tennis ball, which will strengthen the muscles instead of weakening them.

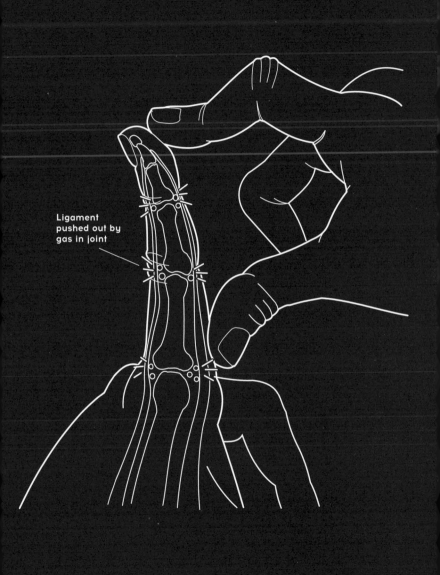

Ligament
pushed out by
gas in joint

DANDRUFF ▶ DUST

Dead skin cells

Hair follicle

DANDRUFF

See also *Dust Coating Your Computer Monitor.*

That little itch could be telling them you have dandruff. Or it could be the fact that your shoulders look like ski slopes, or that you have a bald spot from unremitting clawing at your scalp . . .

Dandruff is very common – about 50 per cent of the world's population suffer with it at some point in their lives. Dermatologists have come to discover that it may be yet another problem caused by an imbalance in the ecosystem of tiny creatures that live on your body. Your scalp is home to a yeast-like organism called *Pityrosporum ovale* (*P. ovale* for short). Climate, hormones and other factors can provide a more fertile landscape for *P. ovale*. Some people's skin overreacts to the presence of these guys. The immune system kicks in and responds by overproducing skin cells which are renewed up to ten times faster than

D normal. Some scientists, however, think the greater presence of *P. ovale* is the effect, rather than the cause of the increased skin production.

Whatever the cause, the more skin cells are made, the more shed. You are always shedding skin, about 400,000 particles a minute, but the skin cells that fall from other parts of your body are so small we only notice them when they accumulate on our computer screens as dust. Your scalp produces more oil than other parts of your body. This binds the skin particles together, producing flakes.

The ICR Survey Research Group (now SSRS) of Pennsylvania questioned 700 people with dandruff. About 21 per cent of those surveyed said they would rather have a headache than dandruff. Another 17 per cent would take heartburn over dandruff. Ten per cent said they would be happier during an allergy attack, and 9 per cent said they would gladly exchange it for athlete's foot.

If your dandruff is less pronounced, you are still probably embarrassed about it, thanks to television adverts that tell you you're supposed to be. Half of the survey respondents were self-conscious about it. Men, it turned out, worried more than women – 58 per cent of the men and 48 per cent of the women were as concerned about what other people think as they were about the condition itself.

If you are worried about your wintry shoulders, dandruff shampoos do work. In fact, a recent study showed that over-the-counter dandruff shampoos were as effective as prescription dandruff shampoos. (This is good because it means the over-the-counter stuff is as effective as anything else, but bad because, if Head & Shoulders doesn't cure your case of dandruff, there's not really anything much better out there.) The main ingredients in dandruff shampoos are zinc pyrithione, selenium sulphide, salicylic acid and coal tars. The active ingredients either retard cell growth (cytostatic) or they loosen and remove cell overgrowth (keratolytic). Some new dandruff shampoos (like Nizirol) employ an antifungal ingredient, ketoconazole, which kills *P. ovale.*

DEAD PENS

D

You are listening to your favourite radio station when the announcer says, 'In just a moment we will give out the telephone number and one lucky caller will win one million pounds.' You grab a pen and the announcer starts rattling off digits. You run the pen across the paper but nothing comes out. You draw circles and squiggles. You tear a hole in the page but still no ink. By now the announcer is saying, 'Congratulations! You're our tenth caller!' You could have been a millionaire were it not for a ballpoint pen malfunction. Bleeping pens!

Before you curse that implement any further, take a moment to appreciate just what a revolutionary invention the pen was. You could have been looking for a knife to sharpen the end of your quill when that contest was announced. László Bíró's 1938 creation combined a ball bearing and fast-drying ink, eliminating the need for messy ink wells or cartridges. In fact, there is an entire book on this groundbreaking invention, *Ballpoint* by György Moldova.

D Now that you've pondered the miracle that is a working ballpoint, here are a few suggestions to fix its non-working counterpart. First, open the cap on the back of the pen and slide the cartridge out to make sure there is actually ink in it. If there is no ink, none of the other tips will do you any good.

One of the most common problems is a ball that has become stuck. If drawing circles fails to get the ball moving, try tapping the tip on a hard surface. This brings the ink down to the point and helps loosen the ball. If that doesn't work, heat the tip of the pen with a lighter. Be sure to keep the tip over the flame for only a couple of seconds, otherwise you might melt the pen. Another method is to dampen a bit of kitchen paper with rubbing alcohol and wipe the tip of the pen to remove any dried ink.

Sometimes the problem is not a stuck ball but air pockets between the tip and the inkwell. You can solve this problem with centrifugal force using a fun helicopter method. Place the pen in the centre of a rubber band. Tape the band to the side of the pen, so that the pen is inside the circle. Using your index fingers, pull on both ends of the rubber band then flip the pen so the rubber band winds up. When it is well wound, release the pen and let it spin to redistribute the ink.

This is also something you can do to keep from getting bored during business calls. If your boss walks by, just say that you're trying to get the ink flowing.

Incidentally, have you ever noticed that a lot of plastic pen lids have a hole at the top? This design feature was implemented to increase air flow – yours. You see an awful lot of people mindlessly chewing or sucking on the ends of their pens. No one has studied exactly how many of us do this, but they do know that about one hundred people a year die after they have accidentally swallowed the things. Pen makers responded by putting holes in the top to allow air to pass even if a lid becomes lodged in the throat. Pen makers are lifesavers. Now, don't you feel bad about complaining?

D

DOGS SNIFFING YOUR PRIVATES

See also *Cats Shredding Furniture*.

You have planned your dinner party for months. You have invited a potential new client and her husband. You spent hours cooking, setting the table with the best dinner service, the soft music is playing and you open the door only to have Fido make a beeline for your guest's privates and nestle his nose right between her legs.

Why does your dog embarrass you this way? Instinct. It is perfectly normal dog behaviour. (As, incidentally, is humping other dogs, inanimate objects and your leg. The American animal charity ASPCA has a web page devoted to 'Mounting and Masturbation' if you want to know more about that.) Fido is not trying to be rude. He probably thinks you're the impolite one when you push him away as he is trying to get to know your guest. A dog's strongest sense is smell. When one dog encounters another, he sniffs around to get information the way you or I would scan someone's face. We look for fine lines and wrinkles to determine a person's age, at their hairstyle and facial characteristics to determine gender, and a whole host of visual cues to tell us about someone's mood. Dogs can glean all of that with a quick whiff.

D   We can't because we lack the receptor cells known as the vomeronasal organ, or Jacobson's organ, that your dog has just above the roof of his mouth. It has ducts that open to the mouth and nose and convey information to the brain thanks to a rich network of blood vessels and nerves. The dog's brain has a much more developed olfactory bulb to interpret this wealth of information.

The sweet spot for smelling is the apocrine gland, a sweat gland that produces pheromones. These are highly concentrated in mammals' genital and anal regions. And if this was not humiliating enough, there are certain scents that are almost guaranteed to draw extra canine attention. In case you think I am making an unwarranted assumption here, you should know that scientists have tested this. In a study titled 'Behavioural Variability of Olfactory Exploration of the Pet Dog in Relation to Human Adults,' Filiatre et al. tested whether dogs were really more interested in the scent of strangers or whether their owners had trained them to keep away from their private parts. They dressed up dolls with clothing worn by a familiar person and to an unfamiliar person. The dogs consistently gave more attention to the unfamiliar scent than the familiar. The researchers concluded that ignoring owners' genitals was not a learned behaviour.

Dogs are especially drawn to the privates of people who have recently had sex, who are menstruating or who have recently given birth. They are also able to detect ovulation. A team of Australian researchers trained dogs to identify cows that had recently ovulated in order to help farmers successfully breed them.

Canine genital sniffing makes us blush a little, but most of us understand that this is instinctive behaviour. Some people, however, are absolutely mortified when it happens. Once a Connecticut woman sued the owner of a Golden Retriever named Kodak for sexual harassment after Kodak sniffed under her skirt. Her lawyers argued that the owner was complicit because he did nothing to stop it. The case was dismissed. As the judge later told a reporter, 'Impoliteness on the part of a dog does not constitute sexual harassment on the part of the owner.'

Kitchen tap

Leaky washer

DRIPPING TAPS

Drip. Drip. Drip. Drip. It's water torture. Pure water torture.

That is, if you're a woman. You probably have conversations that go like this: 'Honey, I thought you said you were going to fix that tap?' 'Yeah. I'm going to get around to it. What's the big deal?' 'Isn't that dripping driving you crazy?' 'I said I'd get to it, didn't I?'

'A dripping faucet [tap] falls into a class of aggravating things that is more aggravating to women than to men,' says Francis T McAndrew, Professor of Psychology at Knox College in Galesburg, Illinois. 'They notice them quicker and are bothered by them more. A man is more likely to say "what noise"?'

The sound of water itself is not irritating. In fact, the sound of a waterfall or a babbling brook is relaxing; but you'll never find a New Age 'nature sounds' CD with the title 'tap drip'. The dripping tap, unlike the waterfall, is a sign that something is wrong. It's the constant reminder

D that something in the home is broken. 'It nags at you because it's not supposed to be there,' McAndrew says. 'It's a signal that there's something amiss and you can't quite relax and forget about it because there's something that needs to be fixed or water's being wasted or whatever is bothering you.'

As to why women are more bothered than men, McAndrew speculates that it has to do with our 'hunter-gatherer' roots. 'Women and men are just primed to tune into different things,' he says. 'There is quite a bit of evidence that women are much better at remembering the location of objects. The hypothesis is that women were the gatherers so they were better at remembering the locations of things.' Presumably, they are tuned into the little things that are amiss in the home environment, like that infernal dripping tap.

Static-electric field between monitor and person

Dust

Computer monitor

DUST COATING YOUR COMPUTER MONITOR

See also *Dandruff*.

Why is it that, no matter how many times you get up and wipe off the screen, you are always running your spreadsheet program through a haze of dust?

Technically, there isn't really such a thing as a 'dust molecule'. Dust can be just about anything as long as its particles are small enough to be carried through the air – less than one-tenth the width of a human hair. Dust is everywhere. It lands on every surface on just about every part of the planet.

Dr Joseph Prospero, a professor of atmospheric chemistry at the University of Miami, has been studying dust for more than 30 years. His discoveries may give you a new appreciation for the snowy coating on your monitor.

Outdoor dust is made up largely of particles of rock that take to the air as wind and water erode mountains. Prospero found that the red dust that fills the air in many East Coast states of the United States

D comes all the way from Africa. Bermuda's islands would not have top soil were it not for blowing African dust. Some terrestrial dust even comes from outer space; it is deposited into our atmosphere by comets and brought home by gravity.

Indoor dust is a different matter: some is tracked in from the outside, but most is created in the house. About 18kg (40lb) of dust accumulates in the average household each year. As you may have heard, most of it is made up of your own skin. Human beings shed about 400,000 particles a minute according to chemist and dust expert Armin Clobes.

Clobes is a senior research associate for SC Johnson Wax. He uses electron microscopes and lasers to analyse the content of household dust. Our dust is a microscopic version of everything we keep in the home – carpet fibres, food particles, dead insects, hair, pet dander and clothing lint.

Given the right conditions, dust can even create dust. If there is enough moisture in the air, mould and bacteria grow in piles of dust and create their own dust clouds. All of this is enough to make the housekeeper throw in the towel, but it is important to try to keep household dust at bay. It provides food for dust mites, a distant relative of the spider. Their waste products can trigger allergic reactions.

Electronics like your computer, television and stereo carry an electric current that generates a field of static energy. Because most dust particles carry an electrical charge, they cling to other charged surfaces. (Sometimes they cling to each other and form dust bunnies.) A dust particle that might just fall off a table sticks to an electronic device because of this attraction.

According to *Electronic Design* magazine, the trajectories of the charged dust particles are influenced by the electric fields between a television or computer monitor and the viewer. Thus, the same coating you see on the screen can accumulate on your face. When you walk away, however, the electrical field is broken and some of the dust will fall off. And you do wash your face more often than you clean your monitor, don't you?

EARS POPPING

EARS POPPING IN AEROPLANE

See also *Aeroplane Legroom, What Does It Cost?*

The plane heads up into the clouds and suddenly you have the sensation of cottonwool being shoved into your ears – from your skull out. The pilot is giving a safety message, but to you it sounds like the adults in a *Peanuts* cartoon. If you have a cold, you're treated to pain as well.

Fast changes in altitude make your ears feel puffed up and blocked. Scientists have a name for this – they call it barotitis or aerotisis. At sea level, the air pressure in your middle ear is equal to the air pressure that surrounds your head. The higher you go, however, the lower the air pressure becomes. So air flows out of the ear through the Eustachian tube and into the nose and throat.

When the plane stops ascending and levels off, your body has a chance to put things back into balance by letting out enough air so your ear pressure matches cabin pressure. Your ears feel fine again until it's time to land. The whole process is reversed as the plane goes down and the air pressure in the cabin increases. Now there is a greater pressure outside than inside your middle ear. The air tries to force its way back into the ear through the Eustachian tube. If it has trouble, say you have a head cold that irritates the tiny tube and keeps it shut, you may feel pain.

The best way to keep barotitis at bay on the way up is to equalize ear pressure by swallowing. It opens the Eustachian tube and makes it easier for the extra air to escape. This is why people suggest chewing gum. Sipping water or chewing on a snack can serve the same purpose. If that doesn't work, *Prevention* magazine suggests swallowing while holding your nose. This creates a small vacuum that draws pressure from the middle ear.

When you head back down, *Prevention* suggests gently blowing air into your nostrils while holding your nose. This technique has a name – the Valsalva manoeuvre. It forces air into the middle ear.

FARTS

Y ou digest, you create wind. Simple as that. Everyone does it – an average of ten times a day. Certain foods are infamous for their wind-producing ability. Beans, broccoli, cabbage and apples contain complex sugars that can't be broken down by digestive juices. Bacteria in the intestines ferment them and the result is wind. You will be pleased to know that scientists have devoted a great deal of mental energy to the study of farts. In 1967, for example, the New York Academy of Sciences held an entire two-day conference on the subject of gastrointestinal wind. A pair of Australians, gastro-enterologist Terry Bolin and nutritionist Rosemary Stanton, wrote a book, *Wind Breaks*, on the subject. It is now in its third printing.

The top researcher today is probably Dr Michael Levitt, chief of research at the Minneapolis Veterans Administration Hospital, who has been studying our emissions since 1965. He has learned that some people pass wind more often and others pass larger volumes less often, but the total volume remains roughly the same, up to 2,000 millilitres, or about 120 cubic inches of wind a day. Frequency depends on the

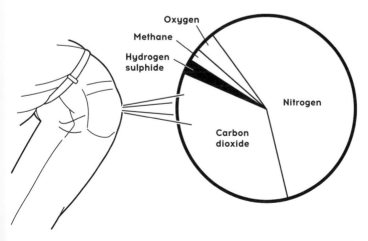

sensitivity of the walls of the rectum. The more sensitive it is to distension the more frequently it will release the emissions. With age, the bowel becomes less elastic and more sensitive to being distended, thus older people fart more frequently, but continue to have the same overall output of wind.

Most of it is odourless. Only 1 part in 10,000 is stinky. It is primarily made up of nitrogen, oxygen, carbon dioxide, hydrogen and methane. The first two ingredients are swallowed while eating. When you burp it is mostly made up of these swallowed gases so it doesn't smell as bad as the stuff that comes out the other end.

The rest of the ingredients in intestinal gas are produced in house. Half of it comes from what we eat. The rest comes from our bile and the mucus and linings of the intestines. Levitt and his team dressed volunteers in wind-tight Mylar pants and collected their gaseous output then filtered it until the subjects reported it no longer smelled bad. They learned that the distinctive smell comes from hydrogen sulphide, methanethiol and dimethyl sulphide. Sulphur is the key ingredient in all of them.

If you have ever described a particularly nasty fart as 'lethal', you were not that far off. The gases are similar chemically to the odorant added to natural gas so we can detect leaks. The brain apparently has the same thing in mind when it reacts to the fragrance. The sulphur-based gases are highly toxic, Levitt says, so we have evolved to detect them at very low levels. The brain perceives the scent as offensive so we try to get away from it. You don't have to tell me twice.

fingernail

slate
chalkboard

FINGERNAILS
ON A BLACKBOARD

See also *Off-key Singing*.

The world is full of annoying sounds – crying babies, car horns, bagpipes and didgeridoo concerts – but the king of them all has to be the sound of fingernails on a blackboard. It is so universally despised it has become a metaphor for awful noise and anything that frays the nerves. What makes the high-pitched scrape so difficult to hear? Believe it or not, scientists have devoted a fair amount of attention, energy and resources to this perplexing question, but they have yet to come to a consensus.

Researchers Lynn Halpern, Randy Blake and Jim Hillenbrand of Northwestern University investigated the 'psychoacoustics of a chilling sound' by having 24 adult volunteers listen to noises and report their reactions. As expected, the subjects almost all cringed at the blackboard sound. The research team suspected that it was the high-pitched portion of the sound that made listeners shiver. They filtered it out and played the remaining sound to their subjects. To the researchers' surprise, they discovered that the volunteers still found the sound unpleasant. Interestingly, when they removed the lower pitched portion of the sound, the volunteers didn't mind it.

William Yost, president of the Parmly Hearing Institute at Loyola University, speculates that the reason people found the second recording bearable was that they no longer recognized it as fingernails on a blackboard and that it is the image of actually running one's fingernails down the slate surface of a blackboard that creates the discomfort, not the sound itself. The Northwestern team has its own theory. They compared the wave forms of fingernails on a blackboard with those of the warning cries of macaque monkeys. They found there was a strong resemblance. Randy Blake wrote in *Psychology Today*, 'We speculate that our spine-tingling aversion to sounds like fingernails scraped over a surface may be a vestigial reflex.'

FLAT BEER

See also *Biscuit Mush, Coffee Spills.*

I t was so refreshing, that first sip of frothy, cold beer on a summer afternoon. Now it's warm and bitter with nothing but a little white circle on top where the foam used to be.

Beer is fizzy because of carbon dioxide, which is generated either by the action of yeasts and sugars in the drink or added at the brewery. In a can, bottle or keg, the CO_2 is kept inside because of the pressure of the container. When the container is opened, the pressure drops and gas escapes.

F

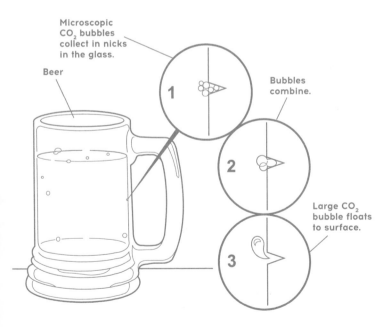

Microscopic CO_2 bubbles collect in nicks in the glass.

Beer

1

Bubbles combine.

2

Large CO_2 bubble floats to surface.

3

F

If you pour your beer into a glass, or if it is contained in a sufficiently clear bottle, you will see tiny bubbles rising to the top in streams along the inside of the glass surface. The bubbles seem to emanate from invisible points. Even though the glass appears to be smooth, the surface has tiny nicks and crevices in it. These hold air pockets, which attract molecules of carbon dioxide. Carbon dioxide is attracted to both the liquid and the air pocket, so it is suspended there for a time. Finally, the air pocket wins out and CO_2 molecules cling together along the surface of the crevice. Once the bubble becomes too buoyant to be held down, it breaks away and rises to the surface and a new bubble starts to form.

At the top of the liquid, the bubbles form foam – the head on a mug of beer. Eventually, the bubbles burst and the head collapses. The bubbles burst faster if they come into contact with fat. Lipstick and the oil on your skin can thus deflate the froth.

Cold liquids can hold more carbonation than warm liquids, so as your beer warms up, its ability to hold CO_2 decreases. More of the gas escapes to the surface and dissipates. Eventually there are no bubbles left.

A team of researchers from the Institute of Food Research (IFR) in Norwich and Brewing Research International in Redhill, Surrey, have taken on the vital task of beer-head preservation. The scientists are studying some of the proteins in barley (an ingredient in beer) that protect the plant from attack by pathogens. 'It was something of a surprise to discover that they might also prove very useful in counteracting the effects of crisp-eating on beer foam,' an IFR press release said.

The team discovered that some of these proteins contain a pocket that can 'mop up' fat molecules and keep them from bursting the foam bubbles in beer. Once they figure out exactly how the process works, they hope to be able to make recommendations on brewing methods to keep you in suds.

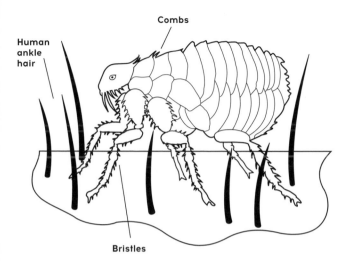

Combs

Human ankle hair

Bristles

FLEAS

See also *Ants, Flies, Gnats and Midges, Mosquitoes.*

Fido's foes are all over your house. The dog is scratching its fur off. You can't walk through the carpet without little insects jumping at your heels. Need any more reason to hate fleas? How about this – their mass-murdering ancestors killed off a quarter of Europe's population by spreading the bubonic plague during the Middle Ages. There are about 1,600 species of flea in the world. The medical entomologist John W Maunder once said he has evidence of a 'vast flea epidemic' throughout Western Europe and much of the United States. In all, the world's fleas probably weigh more than the world's humans. If your cat has fleas, there may be only a dozen or two on the animal. Another 10,000 may be hiding out in the carpet waiting for a warm-blooded host to walk by.

All are tiny, wingless insects with a taste for blood. Their bodies are fortified with a row of spines above their mouthparts (on their back).

These are called the combs or ctenidia. Entomologists used to believe that these helped the fleas move through fur or feathers. Now they believe the setae, bristles on the legs, help them move while the combs make it difficult for you to pluck them out of your pet's fur. If you have ever tried to do this, you've seen first-hand how effective they are. Fleas' hard, pointy heads are perfect for burrowing, and their mouthparts allow them to pierce skin and suck blood.

They measure between 1 to 10mm (0.04 to 0.4in) in length. Don't let their diminutive size fool you – they're strong. If you had the jumping ability of the flea, you could leap to the top of a 25-storey building in a single bound – 30,000 times in row. (Men: if you were 'hung like a flea', you'd have a pair of penises.) Some fleas are picky eaters, preferring the blood of only one species, but others will snack on another creature if their preferred host is unavailable – cat fleas fall into this category. Fluffy's fleas will bite you in a pinch. The most popular mammals, though, are rodents. Fleas love rats. They're not nearly as fond of horses, monkeys, apes and humans.

Flea's eggs are the size of a pinhead. If your pet is infested, you can probably see them in the fur. They look like specks of dirt. When they hatch, Mum and Dad feed the larvae with their blood-rich faeces (yum!). If their parent's droppings aren't available, they eat one another. The larva make cocoons and, depending on the species, they stay there for a few days or months. Then they emerge as fully grown adults, ready to suck some blood.

No fleas in your home? You can look at them in a museum. The largest flea collection in the world is housed in the British Museum in London. There are also collections at the Canadian National Museum in Ottawa and at the Smithsonian in Washington, DC.

FLIES

See also *Ants, Fleas, Gnats and Midges, Mosquitoes*.

I t buzzes around your ear, taunting you. It knows you won't get it with that swatter. You swat, swat, swat and it just laughs at you with that little fly bzzzzz. The reason the fly always seems to get away is that its compound eyes give the insect the ability to respond to light ten times faster than we can. It sees that swatter coming and flies away with wings that beat about 180 times a second (that's also what causes the buzzing sound).

Are you ready to give up and move to Iceland? Forget it – the common housefly, *Musca domestica*, flies EVERYWHERE there are human beings. They're in Iceland and in deserts. One rubbish bin may serve as a breeding ground for more than 30,000 maggots a week. (Nope, they're not even cute as babies.) Depending on which expert you ask, there are between 120,000 and more than a million different kinds of fly in the world. They can walk upside down on ceilings with glands on their feet that produce a sticky substance.

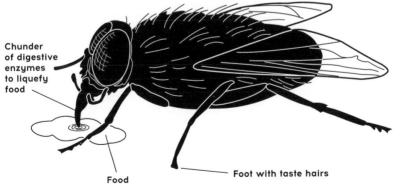

Chunder of digestive enzymes to liquefy food

Food

Foot with taste hairs

Flies can also taste with those feet. They have 1,500 taste hairs, which can savour the flavour of a sugar cube or a cow pat, two fly favourites. To be fair, flies don't actually eat dung. That would be disgusting. They drink the moisture from it. This is because flies urinate every few minutes and they need to take on fluids regularly.

Adult flies can't chew. They sponge up food. That means that they have to convert whatever they eat into liquid. They do this by throwing up. Put another way, they expel digestive enzymes onto food to start breaking it down before they eat it. Then, with the help of a pumping organ in their head, they suck up the liquid using a sponge-like mouthpart. If you're not sufficiently irritated by flies now, here is yet another reason to dislike them: flies have been known to carry such diseases as typhoid fever, cholera, dysentery, trachoma and anthrax, which they spread with their unique feeding habits.

There is one piece of good news about flies. Baby flies – that is maggots – have medical uses. As creepy as the idea may seem, many doctors are using the larvae to eat away dead infected tissue from wounds. They eat the infected tissue while sparing healthy tissue. There is also evidence that maggots exude antibacterial chemicals such as allantoin. Doctors put a quantity of maggots – from a dozen to a hundred or so – into an infected wound and keep them in place with a dressing designed to protect intact skin from the potent enzymes produced by the maggots. An average dose of larvae can digest around 14 grams of dead tissue a day. Yum.

FOOT'S ASLEEP AND FOOT CRAMP

See also *Aeroplane Legroom*.

You have been sitting for a while when . . . pins and needles . . . pins and needles in your foot. If your foot is asleep, it must be having nightmares. Feet do not 'fall asleep' because the circulation has been cut off. If your circulation is interrupted, the result is a leg cramp. A foot falling asleep is irritating. A leg cramp is painful. What happens during a cramp is that a calf or foot muscle goes into spasm and shuts down the blood flow, depriving muscles of oxygen.

A sleeping foot has nothing to do with your veins. A foot usually falls asleep when you have been sitting cross-legged. The peroneal nerve, which runs through the knee and sends messages from the foot to the brain, becomes compressed. As a result, your brain gets all kinds of weird messages about the 'foot', which is actually perfectly fine. People often stand and stomp their feet trying to 'restore circulation'. It does work, but not for the reasons they think. By standing you stretch the nerve back to its normal shape and the odd signals stop.

Peroneal nerve

Tingling sensation

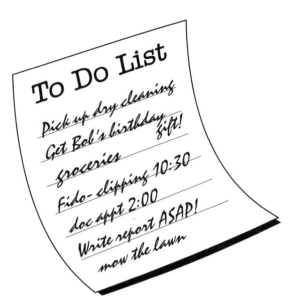

F

FREE TIME? WHAT FREE TIME?

I can't talk now, I have to pick up the kids and take them to band practice and cook dinner and work on my report for tomorrow's annual meeting and mend my jacket and learn French and . . . wait, a text just came in from my boss, he wants me to send off that report to a client in Tokyo . . .

As late as the 1980s forecasters were predicting that by 2000 our biggest problem would be what to do with the almost unlimited leisure time technology would grant us. By 1999 the tune had changed. That year, an issue of *American Demographics* magazine predicted that: 'The cry of the needy in the new millennium may well be "Brother, can you spare some time"?'

In the new century something even more damaging to free time occurred. Our home computers became laptops and then phones, pads and watches. You can always be reached, and the boundaries between home and work, holiday and responsibility began to blur.

Some experts believe that we are not actually any more pressed for time than previous generations – we just believe we are. Time-use experts John P Robinson and Geoffrey Godbey's book *Time for Life* asserts that Americans have almost five hours more free time per week than in the 1960s. In fact, they average about 40 hours of free time per week (away from work, meals, housekeeping chores, child care and sleep). Yet most estimate they have about 16 hours a week of free time.

As people feel more stressed, they tend to misreport the length of time at work to a greater degree. They use 'lack of time' as a shorthand for feeling stressed. Godbey believes that we feel more rushed because 25 of our 40 hours of leisure time fall on weekdays and come in chunks of an hour or two, he claims. 'In many cases, that time does not provide for psychological release. If leisure means tranquility, these hour-long chunks may not have much effect.'

Constant device checking does not help. At work, one study found that 70 per cent of emails were opened within six seconds, and it took a minute per interruption for the recipient fully to regain concentration. That might be OK if we left work at work, but we don't. A survey conducted by Adobe Software found that 87 per cent of employees check emails outside of work. Another survey found that 61 per cent of us do work while on holiday. Yet another survey, this one by a mobile-software firm, found that 68 per cent of people checked work email before 8am, 57 per cent checked on family outings, 38 per cent at the dinner table and half of us check email even in bed. On average, we spend about 6.3 hours reading and responding to emails each day. If you are checking work emails during ad breaks, at the petrol station or when you're waiting for the film to start, your leisure becomes increasingly fragmented and unsatisfying. Increasingly, when researchers ask, people tell them that they would be willing to earn less money in exchange for more free time.

Another reason for our obsession with time is that, as our roles in society become less rigid, more and more of our position in life is determined by portable skills and credentials. Therefore, to increase our value in our chosen careers and society, we need to chalk up many measurable accomplishments. We want to already have done these things. It's not actually the amount of time that gets us, but the number of things we have to keep track of in our minds. When people in labs are asked to do too many things at once, they show increased tension, diminished perceived control and physical discomfort.

F

Some historians, however, question whether we really even feel more time pressure than our ancestors. Maybe we just believe we do. Alexis de Tocqueville, the French commentator on life in the colonies, observed that Americans were always in a hurry.

'It is an age of nervousness . . . the growing malady of the day, the physiological feature of the age,' said a *New York Tribune* editorial. 'Nowhere are the rush and hurry and overstrain of life more marked than in this much-achieving Nation . . . Inventions, discoveries, achievements of science all add to the sum of that which is to be learned, and widen the field in which there is work to be done. If knowledge has increased, we should take more time for acquiring it . . . For it would be a sorry ending of this splendid age of learning and of labor to be known as an age of unsettled brains and shattered nerves.' The article was written in 1895.

GNATS

Gnat

Gnats' mating ritual

GNATS AND MIDGES

See also *Ants, Fleas, Flies, Mosquitoes.*

Gnats are the kind of insects for which the word 'pest' was invented. Even the *Columbia Encyclopedia* has officially dubbed them 'irritating'. The word 'gnat' actually describes a variety of small, two-winged insects. They are most infamous for their habit of swarming around people's faces on warm summer days. From the gnat's perspective, the swarm is something akin to a singles' bar. As part of their mating ritual, males gather en masse around a recognizable object – a bush, a pole or a person standing in a car park. There they wait for their female counterparts. They are short-lived and have only a few weeks to pass on their genetic code, so they are persistent. Flies, incidentally, congregate around dung for a similar reason. Animal waste is full of bacteria that baby flies (maggots) eat. It is also full of moisture that the adults can drink. Thus, male and female flies meet and mate near dung because it's the perfect spot to lay their eggs.

HAEMORRHOIDS ▶ HITTING THE FUNNY BONE

Swollen
blood
vessels

Pain

Seat

HAEMORRHOIDS, OR 'THANKS, I THINK I'LL STAND'

See also *Hernia Exams, Farts, Yellow Spots on Pubic Toilet Seats.*

Haemorrhoids, or piles, occur when the small anorectal veins (the ones that surround the rectum and anus) become enlarged and swollen. In other words, if you have haemorrhoids, you have varicose veins in rather embarrassing places.

The word comes from the Greek *haemorrhoia* meaning 'a flow of blood'. The way the word evolved suggests that haemorrhoids have haunted humanity since the early days of recorded history. As Dr

William S Haubrich put it in his book *Medical Meanings*, 'because the condition was frequent, the source of the bleeding was referred to, anatomically, as "the haemorrhoidal veins". In other words, the bleeding was named first and then the name was transferred to the source.'

There are two major types of haemorrhoids – external and internal. As the name suggests, external haemorrhoids happen outside the opening of the anus. Internal haemorrhoids are found inside the rectum. The external kind are actually more painful because there is a larger nerve supply there.

Haemorrhoids are caused by pressure in the abdomen, which transmits pressure to the anorectal veins. Sitting for long periods of time can supply this kind of pressure. So can straining bowel movements when you're constipated. Haemorrhoids are common during pregnancy because of the pressure placed on the veins by the enlarged womb. Furthermore, the hormones released during pregnancy tend to relax the supporting muscles, exacerbating the problem. Meanwhile, a woman's blood supply increases during pregnancy, thus raising the pressure within her veins. Not only that, constipation is also fairly common during pregnancy.

Journal of Medical Update recommends against using over-the-counter ointments to treat haemorrhoids. Many of these once relied on 'live yeast cell derivatives' as their active ingredients. The US Food and Drug Administration banned these ingredients as ineffective in 1994, but the companies that made products like Preparation H reworked the formulas with other approved ingredients. According to the journal, these ingredients do not necessarily do anything for haemorrhoids. The best thing to do is to avoid constipation by getting enough dietary fibre and to keep the area clean with baby wipes or witch hazel. To relieve the pain, you may also try a sitz bath. Sit for several minutes in a few inches of water that's as hot as you can handle. It helps improve circulation. Recent studies have demonstrated that the application of nitroglycerine cream, which is commonly used for angina in heart patients, may be beneficial in relieving the pain of swollen haemorrhoids. Just don't sit down too fast.

H

H

Epidermis

Thumbnail

Split cuticle

HANGNAILS

See also *Paper Cuts*.

They aren't nails and they don't hang. A hangnail is actually a split cuticle. The little bit of jutting skin can peel away from the finger leaving the red, raw skin underneath exposed. They hurt. That's how they got their name. It comes from the Anglo-Saxon word *ang* meaning 'painful' and *naegl* meaning 'nail'. Thus, a pain near the nail. Where the 'h' came from is anyone's guess.

The cuticle splits because the skin gets too dry or, on occasion, because of a bad manicure. People may joke about someone crying over a hangnail, but they are much more painful than it seems they should be. Your fingertips are a sense organ – they are the part you most frequently use to reach out and touch something. Therefore, they are full of sensitive nerve endings as well as tiny blood vessels. When you are injured there, the nerves fire like mad. What is more, a hangnail can cause something more serious – paronychia, one of the most common hand infections. If a germ known as *Staphylococcus aureus* gets into the torn skin, it can cause an infection with swelling, tenderness and more pain. As tempted as you may be to peel away that little bit of skin, don't. You are likely to tear the skin even more and open it up to a number of nasty organisms.

Instead, soak hangnails in warm water for about ten minutes twice a day. Use manicure scissors to trim off any sharp, dried skin around the edge of the nail. Then rub petroleum jelly over and around the nail and leave it on overnight. The goo will trap moisture and soften the dry skin underneath.

H

HERNIA EXAMS

See also *Haemorrhoids*.

H

Is it really necessary to 'turn your head and cough', or does the doctor just say that to distract you from what he's doing down there? The word 'hernia' comes from the Greek *hernos* meaning 'sprout'. It was so named because the unsightly bulge of a hernia resembled the bud of a plant. In inguinal hernias, the kind your doctor is checking for, protruding tissue descends along the canal that holds the spermatic cord. Some children are born with small gaps in the abdominal tissue. Other people acquire them through overexertion as in jumping, lifting heavy weights or violent coughing. Women can also get hernias, but they are more frequent among men because of their greater physical exertions and because the canal for the spermatic cord leading through the abdominal wall is wider than the canal for the round ligament in women.

Sometimes hernias can become so large that loops of the intestine can slide through, but smaller hernias pose a greater danger because a loop of the bowel can become pinched and obstructed. Small hernias are often not detected by the patient. For the doctor to be able to feel a gap, he needs to get the patient to increase the pressure in the abdomen and cause the hernia sac to bulge outwards. Coughing does the trick. It causes the abdominal muscles to contract and creates the needed pressure.

So why do you have to turn your head? The doctor doesn't want you coughing in his face. The good news is that most patients only have to put up with the test once a year. In the first edition of this book, I concluded by saying, 'Next time you get into a debate about the worst possible jobs, however, you might win by mentioning surrogate patients. Many medical schools now offer urogenital teaching associate programmes to show students how to make patients more comfortable during the less modest exams.' What I was surprised to find was that a number of readers contacted me to find out how they could get a plum gig undergoing ten to twenty prostate, hernia, rectal, breast or pelvic exams by medical students in a single day. I am told that such positions now pay up to £60 an hour, but I am not a recruiter. Contact your local medical school if you want details.

Abdominal muscle tissue

Small intestine

H

HICCUPS

See also *Coughing in the Theatre.*

H

Everyone is – hic – laughing at your pred-HIC-a-ment, but hic, hic, hiccups hurt. Your friends are running up behind you shouting – BOO! But you don't, hic, get cured. Hic! They're making you jump up and down on one leg and drink from the other side of the glass. Now you look stupid and you're covered in water . . . HIC!

Hiccups have been part of the medical literature since Hippocrates' time. In all those years, doctors haven't quite figured out what makes them happen. (They have, however, come up with an obscure medical term for them: singultus.) They don't help in digestion or anything else that doctors can recognize. They can explain the mechanics of hiccups, however. Hiccups are caused by spasms of the diaphragm. When the muscle's movements get out of rhythm you take in big gulps of air. As your lungs quickly fill, your brain tries to put a stop to it by closing the throat. The vocal cords snap shut. The rush of air creates the 'hic' sound.

There has not been much serious study of hiccups because the phenomenon is usually very brief. One of the few hiccup experts, Dr Paul Rousseau of the Carl T Hayden VA Medical Center in Phoenix, Arizona, says that hiccups can occur in spurts of fewer than seven or more than sixty-three. They generally hit at a rate of four to sixty a minute. In extreme cases, hiccupping is more than a nuisance. Some victims of chronic persistent hiccups have suffered for decades. They have trouble holding conversations or eating anything that takes time to chew. The world record holder in hiccups, according to Guinness World Records, is Charles Osborne of Anthon, Iowa, who hiccupped from 1922 until February 1990. Rousseau came across a few cases of death by hiccups in his research. In 2000 the *Washington Times* reported that two Washington, DC residents were fitted with pacemakers, which delivered electrical impulses to the phrenic nerves in an effort to end years of uncontrolled hic-ing.

According to Dr S Gregory Hipskind, you can cure hiccups by rubbing an ice cube on your neck right around the Adam's apple. Apparently, this blocks the nerve impulses that cause the diaphragm to spasm. There is some science behind some of those home remedies. Breathing into a paper bag forces a hiccupper to breathe in more carbon dioxide, which helps regulate breathing. Sipping water from the opposite side of the glass stretches the neck and stimulates the vagal nerve in the brain that helps in swallowing the breathing.

If you're looking for a more controversial hiccup cure, researchers have found some effectiveness in intercourse to orgasm, digital rectal massage and smoking marijuana. 'Honest, officer . . . hic . . . I am using marijuana for medical reasons . . . hic.'

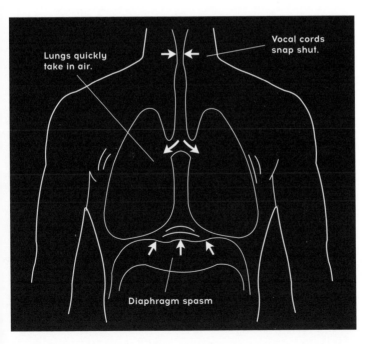

HITTING THE FUNNY BONE: IT'S NOT FUNNY!

I t hurts when you hit the 'funny bone'. It's not funny at all. Not only that, it's not a bone. It's a vulnerable nerve. The ulnar nerve passes behind the humerus in the cubital tunnel, a bony passageway. The nerve controls muscles used for gripping, pinching and fine movement. It's in charge of signalling most of the muscles in your hand with the exception of the two muscles that lift the thumb up.

A lot of sensory information passes along the ulnar nerve between these muscles and the brain. If you hit your arm just there, your brain gets overloaded with signals. You get that 'amusing' tingling, pricking

Ulnar nerve

sensation down the whole length of the nerve to the side of the hand, followed by numbness.

Here's the 'funny' part of the story: clever 19th-century doctors saw the connection between the odd sensation of hitting your ulnar nerve and the 'humerus' and they decided the whole thing was 'humorous' or 'funny'. Thus, funny bone. In the good old days, some people dubbed it 'the crazy bone'.

ICE CREAM HEADACHE ▶ INTERRUPTING

30-60 seconds
of shooting pain

ICE CREAM HEADACHE OR 'BRAIN FREEZE'

What is the most common cause of headaches? Stress? Hangovers? Poor posture? According to Joseph Hulihan of Temple University in Philadelphia, it is ice cream. Hulihan published his findings in the *British Medical Journal* in 1997.

Whether or not you have ever had a migraine, chances are you have experienced the sensation of indulging in a mouthful of Ben and Jerry's only to be rewarded with a sharp pain in the temple. Medical researchers have a name for ice cream headache: they call it 'ice cream headache' (also cold stimulus headache for the more formal among them and sphenopalatine ganglioneuralgia for the absurdly formal). It turns out that migraine sufferers are most susceptible to the phenomenon although US studies show one out of three people have experienced the 30 to 60-second shooting pain of brain freeze. The cause is still a mystery, but you will be pleased to know that scholars throughout the world are working on the problem. One of the earliest brain-freeze researchers was R O Smith, who, in 1968, experimented on himself by moving crushed ice around in his mouth. He learned it was the back of the soft palate that was sensitive to the temperature change.

The researchers disagree on why this gives you a headache. Some theorize that the pain is caused by the rapid cooling of air in the sinuses. Thomas N Ward of the American Council for Headache Education (ACHE – honest) believes that ice-cold 'Cherry Garcia' has an effect on the trigeminal nerve, associated with migraines. Merle Diamond of Chicago's Diamond Headache Clinic blames the glossopharyngeal nerve. Some studies say that you are more likely to experience ice cream headache if you suffer from migraines; other studies reveal the opposite.

J W Sleigh, a senior lecturer at Waikato Hospital in Hamilton, New Zealand, followed up on Hulihan's report by conducting his own study using transcranial Doppler ultrasonography. He measured the speed of cerebral blood flow of three people as they ate ice cream. Two got ice cream headache; one did not. He found that blood flow decreased in the headache sufferers. 'Although the brain temperature was not directly measured,' he concluded, 'these observations suggest that cerebral vasoconstriction causing a decrease in flow may be important in the development of an ice cream headache.'

Research continues. Meanwhile, you can avoid the pain by warming the ice cream in the front of your mouth or putting your tongue against your soft palate to heat it up.

IMPROVEMENTS THAT MAKE THINGS WORSE

See also *Buffering, Computer Viruses, Trolls, Unfriended.*

'For the ways in which technology has not improved the quality of life press one.' They are designed to make life simpler, to make business more efficient, to put an end to extraneous work. Yet nearly everyone has had an experience with a new machine that stops all work in an office for weeks and then slows it down for months while everyone learns it.

Edward Tenner, executive science and history editor at Princeton University Press, calls such things 'revenge effects'. His book *Why Things Bite Back: Technology and the Revenge of Unintended Consequences* argues that our failure to see things as they operate within systems often leads to unforeseen negative results.

The increasing speed of our modes of transportation has had the revenge effect of rapidly increasing the infestation of parasites, rodents and viruses around the world. Our plush wall-to-wall carpets have had the revenge effect of dust mites and allergens. 'Labour-saving' appliances, like vacuum cleaners, can create more work. It is less work to vacuum than to beat a rug but, because we have a vacuum, we feel we must clean more often. Doctors wear surgical gloves to protect patients from germs but, according to the *European Journal of Surgery*, the powder applied to the gloves may cause inflammation, which increases the risk for infection as well as causing false cancer and HIV diagnoses.

Many household products designed to make the living environment cleaner and healthier fill the air with potentially toxic chemicals. New software can have revenge effects of confusion and data loss. 'A machine can't appear to have a will of its own unless it is a system, not just a device,' Tenner writes. 'It needs parts that interact in unexpected and sometimes unstable and unwanted ways.'

The Germans, always economical with language, have a single word for revenge effects – *Verschlimmbesserung*, literally 'worse betterment'.

Related is the Yiddish word *farpotshket*. If you have ever started out with a minor software glitch and, in the course of trying to correct it, wound up completely unable to start your operating system, you have a *farpotshket* computer. The adjective refers to something that is all fouled up, especially through repeated failed efforts to fix it.

Doubt

Improvement

INEFFICIENT PAVEMENT PASS, AKA THE PAVEMENT DANCE

See also *Standing Too Close*.

You are walking down the street. A stranger is coming towards you. You dodge to the left to get out of the way, but he dodges to your left, too. So you correct to the right, just as he corrects to the right. You shift left again, and he shifts. You continue with this awkward little dance until you both plant your feet and verbally negotiate passage.

This little episode plays itself out more frequently in the lives of men than women, but we have all done the pavement dance at some time. We don't talk about it, but passing on the street is a complex social

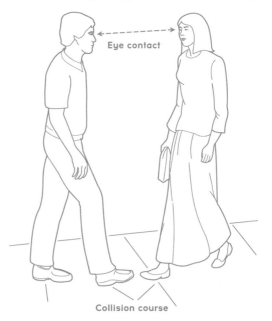

Eye contact

Collision course

interaction with a set of rules and regulations. You will never get a ticket for making an illegal pass on the pavement, but if you stray from the rules you will have some awkward moments or a collision.

Generallly speaking, you are expected to acknowledge someone on the street with eye contact when you are about 2m (8ft) apart. If you spot someone you know coming your way from a distance, you look down and pretend not to see them. If you acknowledge him too soon, you are faced with the embarrassment of having to continue to recognize him for the entire length of a corridor. You must then make all kinds of smiles, gestures and dopey expressions of recognition until you get up to the person to say 'hello'. By that time, you are both feeling so silly that you don't want to be recognized.

When passing a stranger, you communicate your intentions non-verbally at the 2-m mark. You make eye contact, then look at the path where you intend to walk. The other person is supposed to pick up on this and move the other way. If you miss the glance, both glance at once or you don't communicate your intentions in time, you end up miscorrecting. Men collide more frequently than women because studies have shown two men pass at a closer distance than two women or a man and a woman. Some scholars believe men crash more often because they both refuse to yield to the other's wishes.

'Some people have tried to make hay out of this by talking about it as a dominance display, like a game of chicken,' says Francis T McAndrew, Professor of Psychology at Knox College and author of the book *Environmental Psychology*. 'I'm told that in some countries, Mexico comes to mind as one, there's actually sort of a game that men play on the street. They pretend they don't see the other guy and wait for him to move first. If nobody moves and they crash into each other, it doesn't lead to any violence. There are the profuse apologies and everyone goes on their way, but nonetheless, it's sort of one-upmanship about who has to move first.'

If you get into a pavement dance, avoiding eye contact can some-times help. So does loudly announcing, 'I am moving to the right!'

INTERRUPTING, OR 'LET ME FINISH MY SENTENCE OR YOU DIE'

D on't you hate it when – excuse me I was talking – when people interrupt you while you're speaking? 'It's one thing if you interrupt to say "the building's burning down", but if it's not an emergency situation it's very rude,' says Dr Katherine Hawkins of the Elliott School of Communications at Wichita State University, Kansas. 'If I have the floor in a business meeting, and I'm trying to express my point of view and you keep jumping in and negating everything I said, you might just as well have punched me. It's violating an expectation about rules of conversation.'

We are all part of a speech community. As part of this community we know the unwritten rules of conversation. We give each other cues when it's time to speak or time to listen. When you're speaking and another person wants to jump in, she will incline her body forwards, raise her eyebrows and take an audible breath. She's saying, 'I'm taking a breath because I'm about to say something.' If you're not ready to give up the floor, you will avoid eye contact and fill up the gaps in your speech with 'ums' and 'uhs' to keep her from jumping in.

If you have finished speaking, you will signal to her by letting your voice trail off and making eye contact. You may even make a gesture in her direction. There is also something called 'back channel communication'. These are the grunts and noises of encouragement we make while another person is talking. We nod and insert 'uh-huhs' at appropriate intervals. 'This is saying, "I'm listening. This is interesting. Keep talking," but if you speed up the back channel communication it's like saying "Finish your turn. Finish your turn. I want to talk",' Hawkins says.

You might be interested to know that a pushy conversational style not only gets on the nerves of other speakers, it affects the health of the dominating speaker as well. A 22-year study of 750 white, middle-class men carried out by Duke University Medical Center in Durham, North Carolina, ranked the subjects by their behaviour characteristics including verbal competitiveness, loudness and self-aggrandizement. They monitored them taking other health risks into account. The researchers found that those who dominate conversations were 60 per cent more likely to die at an earlier age than their more deferential peers. No word on how many were beaten to death by frustrated people who wanted to get a word in edgeways.

JUNK MAIL

JUNK MAIL

See also *Unsolicited Bulk Email*.

Letterbox

Advertising

Crushed personal letter

Door that does not close

There is a good chance you open your post, if you open it, over the rubbish bin. More than half of what the postal service handles is advertising mail. We call it junk mail. It steals our time and attention, but does not quite make our blood boil like telemarketers or email spam. 'Direct mail lies somewhere in the middle of the nuisance scale,' wrote Cheryl Russel in *American Demographics*. 'Traditional etiquette says that it's rude to interrupt. Advertising that waits to be invited, rather than barging in, is more polite.'

As people have stopped sending handwritten, personal letters in exchange for email and social networking, an increasing percentage of our post is taken up by advertising. The Post Office estimates that about 48 per cent of the mail we receive these days consists of ads. Americans get about 84 billion pieces of junk mail each year. Direct mail advertising has become one of the postal service's main streams of income. Thus, for the past several years, the postal service has been working with direct marketers to increase the amount of third-class mail that comes your way. There is a way to stop it. Under the Data Protection Act of 1998, any organization has to stop using your personal information for marketing purposes if you ask them to remove your details from their mailing list. You can also sign up for the Mail Preference Service, which will stem the tides of junk mail once MPS member companies update their records and learn you don't want to hear from them. But most people don't do this. It turns out that most of us like at least some of the junk we get. What marketers have found is that we hate junk mail, but if we are interested in a particular catalogue or advertisement, we don't mentally categorize it as 'junk'. A lot of it ends up in the recycling, but what doesn't is highly effective. In the United States, direct mail brings in nearly £550 billion a year in sales and employs more than 10 million people. As long as it keeps working, companies will keep sending special offers.

J

KEYBOARD CRUD

KEYBOARD CRUD

See also *Buffering, Computer Viruses.*

First the 's' key stopped working, then the letter 'd'. They are stuck in place by a plaster of biscuit crumbs, skin oil and shed hairs. There may be strange new life forms evolving in there. The more time you spend at your computer, the more sticky and icky the keys can become. As more of us are trying to cram extra hours into our workday by eating lunch at our desk, keyboard crumbs become more and more common.

Keyboard crud makes your work space a little less pleasant, but is easily remedied. You don't need to buy fancy keyboard vacuums or air blowers (although you can if you like gadgets). Many keyboard problems can be avoided by covering the keyboard when it's not in use, especially if your computer is in a home that you share with children.

The crumbs that do find their way into the keyboard can be shaken out. Unplug the keyboard, hold it upside down and shake it firmly about once a week. You can clean the plastic with a soft cloth lightly moistened with cleaner. Spray the cleaner on the cloth, not directly on the keyboard. Coffee on the keyboard? Unplug it right away, turn it upside down and wait for it to dry. That is, if you take your coffee black. Milk and sugar? It's probably time to get a new keyboard, unless you enjoy the smell of sour milk.

K

Coffee

Hand oil

Shred of paper

F

Crumbs

Keyboard

Alt

LATENESS ▶ LIARS

LATENESS

We all have that friend. You know the one: she promised to bring the starters for the dinner party, but arrives in time for dessert. If you want her to be in time for a meeting, you have to lie and tell her it starts 30 minutes before it really does. Does she not value your time? Does she think she is more important than everyone else?

Scientists, it turns out, have devoted a fair amount of energy to the study of the unpunctual. According to one survey conducted in 2006, 15 to 20 per cent of Americans are 'consistently late'. They are eternal optimists, always thinking that things will go more swiftly and efficiently than planned. Put another way, they are incapable of accurately estimating how long tasks will take. The scholarly call this 'planning fallacy' and most of us have a bit of it. Research has shown that people on average underestimate how long a task will take by 40 per cent. While those of us who show up on time compensate for our faulty reasoning, the chronically late do not.

Ron Helpman, a social worker who specializes in tardiness, told *Pacific Standard*, 'There's no single cause. Chronic lateness is a kind of end-product phenomena. People can have very different sorts of motives and patterns that lead them to be chronically late.'

One reason is that they are easily distracted. They are trying to get ready for work, but then they start answering email, and then reading news, and pretty soon they realize they are late, and it is only then that they become motivated. Many latecomers are also champion multi-taskers or, rather, they believe they are champion multi-taskers but they are lying to themselves. A 2013 study from the University of Utah looked at 'plychronicity' – that's what academics call multi-tasking – and found that those who try to multi-task most frequently are, ironically, the worst at it. Many studies have shown that no one is good at multi-tasking, and it is a form of denial to believe that you are.

One thing people consistently underestimate is how long it takes to get from home to work. A 2016 study by Anna Jafarpour at the

University of California at Berkeley and Hugo Spiers at University College London found that the more familiar we are with a geographic area, the more we overestimate its physical size. Interestingly, while we think the territory is larger than it is, we also underestimate how long it will take to traverse the distance. The 25-minute drive becomes, in the mind, a 20-minute drive. Why this should be is a mystery even to the researchers. They hypothesize that there are separate neural systems for estimating space and time to move through space. Or perhaps we judge how long it will take to go somewhere through experience, whereas we judge unfamiliar spaces through the metaphor of the map, which we process differently. In any case, some of us are better at making adjustments for this inherent faulty reasoning than others.

You would think that always suffering the stress of running in at the last minute to glares would make people change. But science tells us that even bad habits form mental pathways in the brain that reinforce behaviour.

So what can you do if you are the one who keeps people waiting? One suggestion is to actually time all of your everyday tasks for a week to give yourself a realistic view of how long things take. Once you have the data, you can add a buffer into your routine and set timers to remind you to start your 'getting ready to go' tasks. I'm sure the unpunctual will get right on that.

LIARS

Can you tell if someone is lying to your face? Don't be so sure. Spotting a liar is tough. In fact, in one classic study researchers pitted trained police officers against university students and had them listen to people telling two lies and two truths. Then they asked them to pick out which statements were lies. The professionals fared no better than the students. The only difference was their level of confidence. Not only were the police more sure of themselves, they became increasingly confident as the study went on.

Liars have a lot of 'tells' but they are not necessarily the ones you may think. What makes them especially hard to detect is that many of them depend a great deal on context. For example, you have probably heard that a liar cannot look you straight in the eye. This is not the case. A man who is lying to another man is just as likely to keep steady eye contact as one who is telling the truth. When a man lies to a woman he actually gazes longer than when he tells her the truth. Women always gaze longer when lying – slightly longer when looking at another woman and much longer when fibbing to a man.

Surely a liar fusses and fidgets, right? It depends. Nervousness and anxiety can make someone fidget and play with objects. How emotional a person gets over a lie depends a lot on her relationship to the other person. Lying to a person with whom you have a strong bond of trust, for example a parent or spouse, will tend to make a person more uncomfortable than lying to a stranger, thus more fidgety. Stress can also raise the pitch of a person's voice. So if someone's voice is high or cracks, he may be lying. On the other hand, liars often become more still as they focus on the details of the falsehood.

People try to give themselves psychological distance from a lie. Liars use the pronouns 'I' and 'me' less often. If a dating ad says 'I love reading', it is more likely to be true than if it says 'Currently reading the complete works of Shakespeare.' Liars also tend to use more negative emotion words such as 'embarrassed' or 'ashamed'.

If you suspect someone is not telling the truth, keep an eye on his nose. When people lie, and feel guilty about it, their blood pressure goes up a bit which boosts blood flow to the tissues in the nose. They stretch and release histamines. The result is an itchy nose, much like hay fever. Your friend may have allergies or he could be a liar.

To catch someone in a lie, ask questions quickly. It is easy enough to make up one lie, but coming up with additional details is harder. Whether they seem thrown or they have a perfect answer for everything, you will have solid clues as to their truthfulness. If you ask someone what he was doing last night, he usually has to pause and think about it. A perfectly rehearsed narrative with no hesitation can tell you you're hearing a whopper.

L

MOSQUITOES ▶ MOTION SICKNESS

MOSQUITOES

See also *Ants, Fleas, Flies, Gnats and Midges.*

There are few things about the mosquito that are not annoying to humans. There is the buzzing, the itching welts they leave behind and their habit of spoiling picnics and barbecues. The fact that they drink blood and in the process transmit disease goes beyond annoying to dangerous.

Mosquitoes, as it turns out, are the most formidable transmitters of disease in the animal kingdom. In various parts of the world they spread malaria, encephalitis, yellow fever, dengue, elephantiasis, the West Nile virus, Zika and dog heartworm. Fortunately, they cannot transmit AIDS. A mosquito that bites an HIV-positive individual does not hold enough of the virus to infect another person. In the United States, only one mosquito in a thousand carries disease organisms, which is a great relief unless you happen to be bitten by the one.

In fairness, it is only a part of the population that gives the rest of the mosquito community a bad rap. Male mosquitoes never bite. It is only the female who sucks blood when she needs the nutrients to develop fertile eggs. The rest of the time, both male and female mosquitoes are satisfied with sugar from plant nectar. Each time a female does snack on an animal's blood, she puts herself at risk of being swatted and killed, so she avoids the blood feast until absolutely necessary.

Humans are not even the female mosquito's favourite choice of host. She prefers the taste of birds, rodents and large mammals like cows and horses. If those delicacies are unavailable, however, she is happy to snack on a person. She knows where you are because you breathe.

A mosquito can detect carbon dioxide from up to 65km (40 miles) away, according to some sources. She localizes a breathing animal by flying in a zigzag fashion across the stream of CO_2. As she approaches, she sniffs for water vapour and lactic acid, which tell her that the source is an animal and not, say, a smokestack. When she gets close enough,

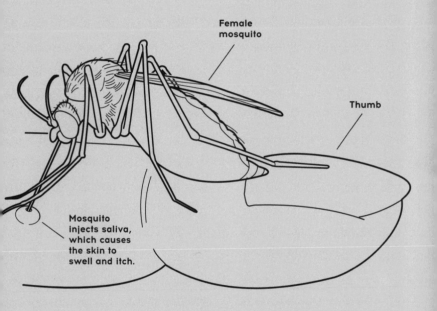

Female
mosquito

Thumb

Mosquito
injects saliva,
which causes
the skin to
swell and itch.

she uses her other senses. She observes movement and detects the infrared radiation emitted by warm bodies.

She has no illusions that you will welcome her visit, so she tries her best to land in a place that is hard to swat – and consequently hard to scratch. Sometimes, though, she gives herself away with the telltale whine of her wings, which beat up to 500 cycles a second. If she does manage to avoid detection, she searches the skin's surface with her stylet until she finds a capillary. Then she punctures the skin with four of her six probes. The other two are then used like a straw to slurp up the blood meal.

Her saliva keeps the blood from clotting and also serves as an anaesthetic, which is important to the mosquito because it takes up to five minutes to complete her meal. The anaesthetic helps her avoid detection. The swollen, itchy welts that appear after she leaves are caused by an allergic reaction to the saliva. It takes about three minutes from the time she bites you for the spot to start itching.

There is a popular myth that if you let the mosquito drink her fill she will remove the anticoagulant before she leaves and the bite will not itch. There is no truth to this, but there is at least one reason to let a mosquito finish. If she has not drank her fill, she may come back. The result is two welts, not one.

If you seem to be a person who is particularly attractive to the pests, there is good news and bad news. The good news is you are not crazy – mosquitoes really do favour the taste of some individuals over others. The bad news is, you are not crazy – mosquitoes really do favour the taste of some individuals over others.

Why do mosquitoes prefer certain people? Well, scientists don't know everything. So far, they are only able to prove that they do. The best way to keep mosquitoes at bay is to rid the environment of their breeding ground – standing water. The mosquito's hunting ground is about 30 to 60m (100 to 200ft) from where she begins her life cycle. If she breeds far away, she'll bite far away, too.

Some swear that high doses of the B vitamin thiamine or garlic pills can make a person unattractive to the pests. For those who prefer to avoid commercial repellants with DEET, there are a number of natural deterrents you can try. Pennyroyal essential oil, peppermint, vanilla, bay, clove and cedar all have their adherents. You could try burning rosemary and sage on your next barbecue – some swear this keeps mosquitoes at bay. Some rub fresh parsley or apple cider vinegar on the skin. Another home-made bug repellant can be concocted with 1 tablespoon citronella oil, 500ml (18fl oz) white vinegar, 240ml (9fl oz) water and 240ml (9fl oz) bath oil.

If none of these preparations works for you, your best bet is to figure out who among your friends is most attractive to mosquitoes and invite them to all your outdoor parties. Be sure they stand near you.

M

7.5 by 12.5-cm
(3 by 5-in)
opening of air
sickness bag

MOTION SICKNESS

See also *Aeroplane Legroom*.

A h, sailing. The fresh sea air. The lapping of the sea against the hull. The rocking back and forth and back and forth and . . . Oh no! Why is it that you can ride your bike without getting sick, but on a boat, or in the back seat of a car, your stomach contents come up?

When you walk down the street you never get walk-sick. But when you are in a big vehicle, especially if you're not driving, things change. Inside an aircraft, for example, the fluid in your ears shifts as the plane rises and sinks. This signals your brain that your body is in motion. Your eyes, however, are telling a different story. They aren't perceiving a lot of movement. They tell your brain that you are in a big room sitting in an uncomfortable chair reading a magazine. This confuses the brain. The brain hates to be confused, so it sends out stress hormones like adrenaline. The stomach is especially susceptible to stress cues and it contracts. With luck you make it to the airsick bag on time.

The best way to avoid motion discomfort is to look out of the window or go up on deck so your eyes will be on the same wavelength as your ears. Avoid reading in a vehicle and don't travel on an empty stomach. It increases queasiness. If you fly, choose a seat over the wing on the right side of the plane. Most flight patterns turn left, so you won't be jostled around as much if you sit on the right.

Then again, if it weren't for motion discomfort, some people would not have a hobby. In recent years collecting air sickness bags has become a thing. The idea of a plastic-lined bag came from Gilmore Tilmen Schjeldahl who offered his invention to the airlines in 1949. Initially, they were used for food storage. Northwest Orient Airlines first realized the bags could be useful in containing the stomach contents of woozy passengers. They quickly became an industry standard.

These days collectors treasure bags from defunct airlines, and curiosities such as bags made out of blotting paper, bags with games on the back, a bag that doubles as an envelope for a film development company, an almost transparent bag, an airline with separate business- and economy-class airsick bags, and even a sack that carries the curious caution: 'When used, this bag may contain biohazardous waste.'

A Dutch collector, Niek Vermeulen, has earned a place in the *Guinness Book of World Records* for his 6,290-piece collection. You can browse the bags from the safety of your stationary office chair via the Air Sickness Bag Virtual Museum (www.airsicknessbags.com). The hobby has taken off to the extent that a Ryanair executive suggested, in 2009, that they might start charging passengers for them. Now, that would be annoying. (See *What Does It Cost? Hidden Fees*.)

M

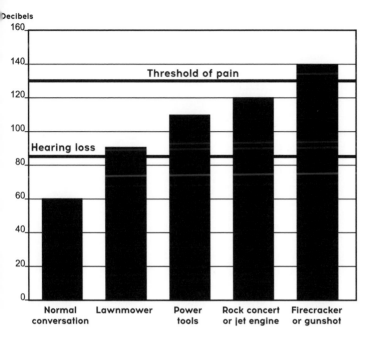

Decibels

160

140 — Threshold of pain

120

100

Hearing loss

80

60

40

20

0

Normal conversation | Lawnmower | Power tools | Rock concert or jet engine | Firecracker or gunshot

NOISE

See also *Car Alarms, Fingernails on a Blackboard, Off-key Singing.*

Your neighbour loves to blast heavy-metal music on his stereo. How can he stand to listen to that noise? You would rather listen to a washing machine that is out of balance. Scientists have attempted to quantify the annoyance factor of sounds with a noise scale, NOY. The problem is that there is little agreement among research subjects as to what is sound and what is noise. Noises are usually loud, for example, but loudness alone does not make a sound annoying to all listeners. A 2013 study in the *Journal of Environmental Psychology* found that the sort of loud, continuous racket that we normally call 'noise' can be experienced as a positive in the right social contexts, such as a religious festival. Other studies have found that we are more bothered by sounds that are incomprehensible than things like speech in our own language, and that intermittent loud sounds are more bothersome than something ongoing, like traffic noise.

'Noise is a psychological phenomenon,' says environmental psychologist Arline Bronzaft. The ear hears but 'it's the higher senses of the brain that determine whether that sound is unwanted, unpleasant or disturbing'. Noise, it seems, is loudness plus annoyance.

What experts generally agree upon is that noise is bad for you. Hearing loss, sleep disorders, elevated blood pressure, heart disease and psychological trauma can be brought on by exposure to noise. One of the earliest studies of noise was conducted in New York City and found that children who live near clattering subway lines have a harder time learning. Other studies have correlated high-noise areas with poor reading and maths scores in school-age children. Two studies conducted near London's Heathrow Airport found that areas closest to the airport, with higher levels of noise, also had the highest rates of psychological hospital admissions. Sudden, unexpected noise causes the heart to race, blood pressure to rise and the muscles to contract. Following a loud bang, digestion, stomach contractions and the flow of gastric juices all stop. Appropriately enough, the word 'noise' is a distant cousin of the word 'nausea'. Both evolved out of the Greek *nautia* and Latin *navis*, or ship. Nausea was originally used specifically to describe seasickness. Eventually, it was applied to similar discomfort on land. The related word, 'noise', was once used in Latin to describe the fuss surrounding a sick person. In Old French it was transformed into an expression for loud disagreement. This term came into English where it was applied to any unpleasant sound.

Researchers at Northwestern University in Evanston, Illinois who studied the sounds that make people cringe found that fingernails on a blackboard was by far the most universally annoying. What was the second most aggravating noise, according to their subjects? It was the sound of two pieces of Styrofoam rubbing together.

NON-APOLOGY APOLOGIES

'I'm sorry if you were offended.'

Never mind that. Are you sorry for what you did? If your remorse is limited to regretting that there was a backlash, then you are not really apologizing. Thane Rosenbaum, author of *The Myth of Moral Justice*, calls this kind of utterance 'the apology of the passive aggressive'.

It is never fun to admit you are not perfect. Public figures are especially prone to spectacular gaffes for the simple reason that more people are paying attention. When they do, they are masters of so-called apologies that contain more excuses and justifications than remorse. Suddenly, they speak in the passive voice: 'Mistakes were made.' Embedded in their apologies is an accusation against the injured parties for misunderstanding or overreacting. 'We're sorry you were inconvenienced but . . .'

No. No but. If you're 'sorry but', you're not sorry!

Politicians are notorious for that sort of thing, and people are finally cottoning on to it. They have invented many terms for the non-apology

apology. You can call it a 'fauxpology', a 'nopology' or the 'past exonerate'. A popular social media hashtag is '#sorrynotsorry'.

Of course, there were reasons you behaved as you did. If you ended up doing something that hurt someone else, they are probably not great reasons. Even if they are ('I was only racing to save a child from a burning building when I ran over your poodle'), now is not the time to bring them up. Your goal is not to save face but to express your regret. Your apology should not be about your feelings, but the feelings of the other person. See the situation from her perspective and use empathy to show you understand how your actions affected her.

Do not try to shift the blame. You end up sounding like a child pointing at another kid in the playground saying, 'He did it.' This is not actually an apology: 'I am sorry I made you cry, but if you hadn't got on my case like that I wouldn't have called you that name.' To apologize you need to accept full responsibility for your actions. No 'ifs' or 'buts'.

Resist the impulse to shift into the second person. This is a place where many apologies go wrong. When you say 'I'm sorry . . . you didn't understand me', you are not apologizing for your actions; you are telling the other person that you are sorry that he reacted the way he did. A real apology begins 'I'm sorry I. . . .'

You are not done. Part of admitting you did wrong is offering some sort of solution to undo what you did. 'I am sorry I broke your vase. Can I give you the money to replace it?' 'I am sorry I hurt your feelings, I will work on my short temper so I don't do that again.' 'I'm sorry I forgot your birthday. Is there anything I can do to make it up to you?'

You must be sincere about changing your ways. If this is the tenth time you have said, 'I'm sorry I didn't call. I will remember to do that next time,' your apology will not be, nor should it be, believed.

If you have really screwed up, do not expect an apology to work like magic. Accept that it may take a while to receive the other person's forgiveness and trust. If the other person does not react the way you would like, do not keep arguing the point. Simply say, 'I understand. Again, I am sorry', and give her some time to cool down.

All of this runs a bit contrary to our culture, especially in Western cultures. Rosenbaum points out '[t]he conventional legal paradigm provides mostly disincentives to apologize and, in most cases, actually discourages it'. By contrast in Japan the president of an airline that has a crash will go to the homes of all of the families and ask for forgiveness.

This seems to work even in the West, although we are loath to do it. Studies have shown that when hospitals apologize for medical mistakes and offer those who were impacted by them solutions including information on how to file malpractice lawsuits, they are actually less likely to sue. People understand that human beings make mistakes, but they want others to take moral responsibility for their actions. Rosenbaum puts it this way: 'One of the dirty little secrets of the legal system is that if people could simply learn how to apologize, lawyers and judges would be out of work.'

N

OFF-KEY SINGING

OFF-KEY SINGING

See also *Car Alarms, Fingernails on a Blackboard, Noise.*

'I go to karaoke night to be spiritually uplifted by the beauty of song', said no one in the world, ever. Music is soothing, fun, joyous – except when Mr Francis Off-Key takes over the mike to belt out a painful rendition of 'Summer Nights' from *Grease.*

Singing is universal. Most children start to sing recognizable tunes by the time they are 18 months old. But a small percentage of the population never really masters it. We call them 'tone deaf', although that is not really an accurate description. Actual tone deafness, an inability to tell the difference between musical notes, is quite rare, affecting an estimated 2.5 per cent of the population. Another term for this condition is amusia. François Lhermitte, who had this problem, told Oliver Sacks that, when he heard music, 'he could say only that it was "The Marseillaise", or that it was not.'

More common is what they call an 'imitative deficit'. Sean Hutchinson, who studies the neuroscience of music, found that the people he studied had no problem recognizing pitch and tone. The problem came when they tried to reproduce it with their voices. The singer hears the right note, but somehow the wires get crossed and the brain associates that sound with the wrong muscle movements in the throat. Instead of singing a C the subject will sing a B-flat. When Hutchinson played the target note for such subjects, they repeated it wrongly every time, and in a consistent way. It was as though the keys on the piano were strung to the wrong hammers.

A Warsaw psychologist, Simone Dalla Bella, identified two general types of poor singer. One group, like Hutchinson's, could not hit the right note no matter how hard they tried. They knew they were not getting it right and cringed at their own attempts at 'Happy Birthday' and 'Jingle Bells'. The second group could not carry a tune in a bucket and remained blissfully unaware of the fact. They are not competent to sing, and yet not competent enough to know they are not competent to sing. It is this group that fills the karaoke bar on a Saturday night.

There are, of course, those rare few who are able to elevate musical incompetence into an art form all its own. There is a certain *je ne sais quoi* that creates a Florence Foster Jenkins, the enthusiastic and pitch-free 1940s crooner who became the subject of a 2016 biopic starring Meryl Streep. It is impossible to put your finger on exactly what this genius is. But the right spirit, a lot of luck, great confidence and a complete lack of self-awareness seem to help.

PAPER CUTS ▶ PUBLIC TRANSPORT

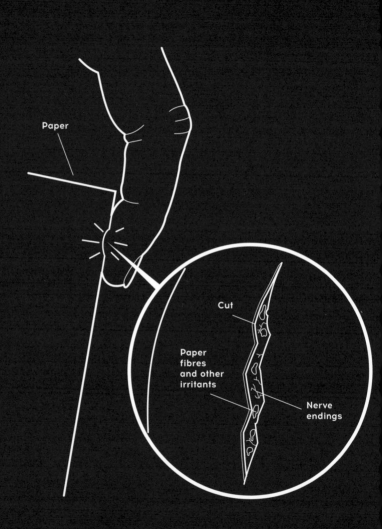

Paper

Cut

Paper
fibres
and other
irritants

Nerve
endings

PAPER CUTS

You are handing a memo to the boss who wants everything in writing when, sliiiicccceeee . . .

It slips past your finger, cutting a gouge as it goes. Why is it that when you cut yourself shaving this morning you didn't feel a thing, but a flimsy piece of paper has you wincing and sucking your finger like a baby?

A razor cuts your skin smoothly and superficially. Paper cuts actually tear through your skin. The cuts are tiny but deceptively deep. As Dr Ted Broadway of the Ontario Medical Association explained to the *Toronto Star*, the cuts 'just get into the layer of the nerve endings and irritates them. The friction of the tissue causes the nerve endings to go nuts. Every nerve is firing.' The paper also contains more irritants than the razor. It leaves fibres and chemicals in the tiny wound.

Some people use superglue to seal paper cuts shut. Doctors have been using a medical-grade superglue to repair skin lacerations for some time. The stuff you find at the DIY store was not specifically designed for the purpose, so you probably should not slather it over large, deep cuts, but dermatologists say it is not likely to be toxic on something as small as a paper cut. If you do try this method, be sure you let the glue dry before you pick anything else up. You definitely don't want to end up with a throbbing, sliced finger glued to a coffee cup.

P

PASSWORDS, OR WHY DOES EVERY SITE HAVE ITS OWN SODDING PASSWORD RULE?

See also *Buffering, Computer Viruses, Improvements That Make Things Worse.*

'efore you log in, you must select a new password.'

'snoopy'

'Not enough characters. Password must include at least eight characters.'

'snoopy10'

'Password must include a combination of letters and numbers and at least one capital letter.'

'Aaaarrggghhh!@#%!!!'

'For security please retype password.'

'What did I type? Wait!'

'Too many log in attempts. You have been locked out. Please call customer service.'

Why is it that every site seems to require its own special password combination? You can't remember all those passwords. Heck, you can't even remember what type of password each site requires. Here is what you need to know about all of those password requirements: we hate them, we are annoyed when systems force us to change them and when we do change them we do so in predictable patterns that researchers are starting to realize may make us more vulnerable to hacking, not less.

A 2015 survey, conducted by a firm that sells password management software, found that one-third of Internet users have at some point suffered from 'password rage', even screaming, swearing and crying when they can't log into a site. They rated forgetting a password more annoying than misplacing their keys or a dead phone battery.

Numerous studies have shown that systems that require frequent password changes only impede hackers for a short time, and that when users are annoyed by having to change their passwords they choose weaker passwords to begin with and they are more likely to write them down somewhere accessible. One survey found that the average user has 27 distinct passwords and that 37 per cent of people forget a password at least once a week. By the way, research shows that one of the most common ways people select a password is to use the name of their pet, so you might cross Fido and Fluffy off your list of clever codes.

Researchers at the University of North Carolina, studying the passwords of defunct accounts where students were required to change their passwords every three months, found that we are pretty predictable. We don't want to have to remember a whole new password, so we engage in what they call 'transformations' such as changing the number at the end by one digit so 'snoopy10' becomes 'snoopy11', substituting a special character for a letter so 'snoopy' becomes '$no0py' or moving the numbers from the end to the beginning so 'snoopy10' becomes '10snoopy'. Once they cracked one old password, it became easy to detect a pattern and find more recent passwords.

According to Lorrie Cranor, a computer science professor at Carnegie Mellon University and an expert on password usability and security, you do not need to change your password unless you have some reason to believe it might have been compromised. If you see someone looking over your shoulder – or as happened to someone I know, you accidentally type it in while your computer is being projected onto a big screen in a full lecture hall – it is time to change not only that password, but all your other ones because, if you are like most people, once someone knows your LinkedIn password they can guess your Facebook password and your bank password.

Of course, it doesn't matter much how hard or easy your password is if it is stored as easily decipherable plain text on a company server. As Donna Dodson, chief cyber security officer for the National Institute of Standards and Technology, told *Wired*, 'Putting the burden of security on the end-user and making it more complex just doesn't work. The security has to be usable for the end-user. Otherwise they're going to find workarounds.' In spite of mounting evidence that our complex password rules are not slowing hackers down, the practice persists. Why? One IT professional confessed to *Wired* that it just feels more secure and if they looked like they were watering down their security, people would protest.

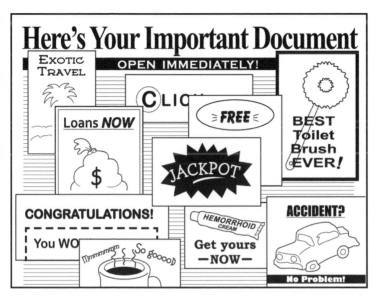

POP-UP ADS

See also *Buffering, Passwords*.

You are browsing your social network of choice when you see a link to a headline that sounds interesting. You click on it, read the first paragraph and just as you are relaxing into the article an advertisement pops up over the text, preventing you from reading until you click to close it.

Some have argued that in the Internet age, people are no longer willing to pay for content, and expect to get everything for free. This is not a fair assessment. We have always got media for free, paid for by advertising. Television and radio were beamed right into our homes, and you could buy a newspaper for 25 pence, far less than the cost to produce it. What has changed is not so much our willingness to pay but the ability to measure whether we look at an ad or not. In the past, there was no good way to know if those subscribers paid attention to the ads, and so marketers would sell ads based on how many papers were sold or how many people listened to the station. Clicking and page loads changed all that.

In the early days of the Internet the standard form of advertising was the banner ad, a rectangular space usually at the top of the page. People became so accustomed to the top portion of any web page being an ad that studies showed experienced Internet users eyes did not even scan that part of the page. It was as though it didn't exist. Advertisers have no interest in wasting their money on ads no one sees. New sites responded by creating ads that pop up and draw your attention. These soon took over because they worked – they were clicked on two to five times as often as static banner ads. Eventually, as we got used to them, advertisers came up with increasingly intrusive ads adding streaming music and video as new broadband connections allowed. The most annoying pop-up is the kind that lets you start to read and then covers the text – argh! Readers responded by inventing the ad blocker, and sites that rely on advertising responded with pop-ups that block you from a site if you don't turn off your ad blocker.

If you are looking for someone to blame, the inventor of the pop-up ad is Ethan Zuckerman. In the mid-1990s, when he was a programmer for Tripod.com, the code for an ad that was separate from the page content was not created initially to make ads annoying and in-your-face. He told the *Atlantic*, 'It was a way to associate an ad with a user's page without putting it directly on the page, which advertisers worried would imply an association between their brand and the page's content. Specifically, we came up with it when a major car company freaked out that they'd bought a banner ad on a page that celebrated anal sex. I wrote the code to launch the window and run an ad in it. I'm sorry. Our intentions were good.'

WINTER

Asphalt

Gravel Bed

Ground

Frozen water

SPRING

Pothole

POTHOLES,
OR 'FASTEN YOUR SEATBELTS,
WE'RE IN FOR A BUMPY RIDE'

See also *Car Park Battles, Road Rage*.

P

There are some roads that seem more like amusement park rides rather than a highway. Your car rises and falls with a ferocity that threatens to puncture your tyres and shake your fillings lose. One of the main causes of potholes is water. As a liquid, water seeps into little cracks in the cement. Then, on cold days, it freezes and when water freezes it expands. This makes the cracks bigger. When the ice melts and takes up less space, it leaves a gap in the concrete and bits fall in. A pothole is created.

If you want the official definition of a pothole, the US Federal Aviation Authority defines it as 'usually less than 750mm (30in) in diameter, bowl-shaped depressions in the pavement surface. They generally have sharp edges and vertical sides near the top of the hole.' They may be small but they cause more than their share of aggravation as motorists head to their local repair centres for new tyres and other costly fixes.

If freezing is the main cause of potholes, then you would expect that colder locations would lead the league table of bumpy rides. Yet, according to research by the national transportation research firm TRIP, the worst roads in the United States are in the fairly temperate Washington, DC. It is followed by sunny California, where 51 per cent of the roads are rated as poor. The two worst cities for potholes are in California. The San Francisco/Oakland area is the worst with 71 per cent poor roads. It is followed by Los Angeles, with 60 per cent poor roads and then by San Jose, Detroit, Michigan and Milwaukee, Wisconsin.

Another cause of potholes is politics. It is hard for a politician to stage a photo op at the site of routine road maintenance. It is easier to do so at a ribbon cutting for a new construction project. As a result, it is new construction that tends to get the tax money. In the United States road repair is funded primarily through taxes on fuel. No one likes to see the price at the pump go up, and no politician wants to be held responsible for causing that. So, as of 2015, the federal petrol tax remained at 1993 levels.

While we are on the subject, here is a pothole trivia question: which Beatles song was partially inspired by potholes? Answer: 'A Day in the Life'. John Lennon frequently took lyrical inspiration from his daily newspaper. The '4,000 holes in Blackburn, Lancashire' came from a report of the Blackburn City Council survey of road holes reported in *The Daily Mail*, 17 January 1967. The survey found that there was one-twenty-sixth of a hole in the road for each Blackburn resident.

PRESBYOPIA,
OR 'NOW WHERE DID I PUT
THOSE READING GLASSES?'

For most people it starts around the age of 40. You pick up a book or a menu and suddenly you find you can't focus on the letters. When someone holds up a piece of paper at the distance from which you would expect to be able to read it, you have to take it and hold it out as far as your arm can reach. You are suffering from middle-aged far-sightedness, or presbyopia.

It happens to the best, and the worst, of us. Did you know Adolf Hitler needed reading glasses? Probably not, because the Nazi Party censored images that showed him wearing them out of fear he would seem weak. Many people are like Hitler to the extent that they do not want to be seen in public with reading glasses dangling from a chain around their neck. Thankfully, that is all they have in common with Hitler. (We can only hope.)

A 2012 study by Israeli and US scientists suggested that certain types of visual exercises might improve the vision of people with presbyopia, but their findings have not yet been tested in a randomized controlled trial, so optometrists remain sceptical. Interestingly, the formation of cataracts can sometimes allow people to read without their glasses, that is, until the cataracts obscure their vision.

The cornea of the eye focuses light through the lens and onto a membrane called the retina. Muscles around the lens relax or contract to either flatten or thicken the lens depending on whether you need to focus on something near or far. As you age, the lens becomes denser and less flexible. The process actually begins in childhood, but it takes a while for you to notice. Then suddenly, it seems, sometime between ages 35 and 45, it gets to the point that the muscles have a hard time flexing the lens enough to see the small print.

Presbyopia is easily corrected with prescription or non-prescription reading glasses, the latter of which you can buy at any pharmacy or even a pound shop. Optometrists usually recommend the prescription kind, as they are made specifically for your eyes. Some eye doctors take a more pragmatic approach.

Reading glasses do not come with standard tracking devices. After a lifetime of not needing glasses, and then needing them only for reading, the damn things are always in another room when you need them. As readers are often misplaced and a £10 pharmacy pair is easier to replace than a £100 prescription pair, some doctors recommend them. One even told the *New York Times* that tall people may not need them at all because they have long arms and can hold the book farther away from their eyes.

Even so, they recommend that you visit your optician either way because the age at which your close-up vision starts to become problematic is also the age when other eye health issues can pop up.

P

PROCRASTINATION

I intended to include this subject in the first edition of this book, but I didn't get around to it. Don't blame me. Blame human psychology. Studies reveal that we're all overly optimistic when it comes to what we will have the time and inclination to do in the future. The scholars call it 'present bias'. That is, you imagine you will happily carry out all of the great intentions you make (but do not start) today. You want to be a person who has read the classics. You believe you will want to be that person just as much tomorrow and therefore tomorrow you will begin reading *War and Peace*.

Even though your present self would rather be playing Angry Birds, for some reason you are fairly certain that your future self will be highly motivated to finish your report, start an exercise plan and learn Spanish.

By the time your future self becomes your present self, you will have discovered a great series of surfing dog videos that you want to alphabetize in your bookmarks and you will be intent on experimenting with a new style of napping.

Face it, you don't know your future self at all. You can track down the best time management software on the market, and read up on how to organize your to-do list. You might even buy one of the more than six hundred books on the market that promise to cure you of your procrastination – and vow to read it tomorrow. These are, in themselves, great ways to procrastinate.

None of this is likely to solve the problem because your future self will simply pass all of the tasks on that to-do list onto your future self until you are up against an immovable deadline. There will always be a more appealing shiny object vying for your attention.

To circumvent this, you need to give every task on your to-do list a deadline. Tell yourself you need it done by Wednesday and vow to stick to it. Then when your Wednesday self sees the task is due, you are much less likely to insist you will do it on Thursday.

People often become overwhelmed by their to-do lists because they expect it to get finished. It won't. When you cross one thing off,

P

there will be a new thing to do. As you can't actually clear the page, you do not have to stress over that.

P   The purpose of a to-do list is to get the tasks out of your short-term memory so you can be more effective. Our brains are unable to hold more than five to nine things at one time. Write down 'go to the post office', and don't worry about it until it's time to tackle that task and cross it off the list.

When you are more aware of the mental games you play to put off tasks, you can come up with better countermeasures. Always remember, if you don't feel like doing something today, chances are you will not be any more inclined to do it tomorrow. If you really want to learn Spanish or read Proust, you might as well start now.

PUBLIC TRANSPORT

See also *Stuck in Traffic*, *Weather*

'It came from the sky; it was white; it looked like the regular stuff. But if British Rail is to be believed, there was something alien about the snow that shawled the country last Thursday and Friday.' That's how the *Daily Telegraph* began an article published in February 1991 after a spell of particularly wintry weather had disrupted the nation's railway service. The Met Office backed up this assertion: 'It came in smaller flakes, which tended to remain separate. Instead of caking together, they were whipped into the air by the icy blast.' The result was frozen points, frozen doors, burned-out motors – and a lot of very cold and aggravated commuters.

The problem with living in a temperate climate is that anything remotely extreme catches us by surprise. In North America and Continental Europe, they put snow tyres and chains on the car and get on with it; in the UK, we cancel buses, shut schools and encourage everyone to stay at home. Though, to be fair, a freakish winter storm on the North American West Coast in the early 1990s revealed that notoriously wet-but-mild Seattle was woefully underequipped with snow ploughs and the city ground to a halt for several days.

Blaming the weather isn't confined to winter, either. If commuters want to avoid aggravation, they should go to work only in the spring. Railway lines may buckle if the temperature hits 35°C (95°F), so during a heatwave strict speed limits are imposed and journeys are subject to that all-too-familiar double-act, delays and cancellation. Then there are the much maligned 'leaves on the line', which recently headed a local paper's list of 'excuses commuters are tired of hearing'. But it is a fact that leaf mulch reduces the friction between wheel and rail which is essential for safe braking. In 2015 a Cambridge-based engineering company called Mole Solutions proposed the use of an 'out of vehicle electromagnetic control loop' to 'ensure the required braking performance is met'. Commuters await the result of their feasibility study . . .

Moving from trains to buses, there's 'nothing for ages, then three come along at once', though mathematicians Rob Eastaway and Jeremy Wyndham have shown that this isn't as common as you might expect. 'Two come along at once' is much more likely. Say buses leave the terminus at ten-minute intervals. The first gets held up at a level crossing. When it reaches the next stop, it has lots of passengers to pick up. By the time the second bus reaches the crossing, the train has passed and it progresses smoothly to the bus stop, where there are fewer passengers waiting because so many have crowded on to bus number one. Of course, number two is going to catch up.

The further along the route you go, the more probable this is, and the more buses there are on the route, the more likely they are to congregate – simply because they were scheduled to be closer together in the first place. In other words, the better your bus service, the more likely you are to find that three do indeed come along at once.

Will the maths make you feel any better when you are standing in the cold wondering if it would be quicker to walk? I doubt it.

P

QUEUES

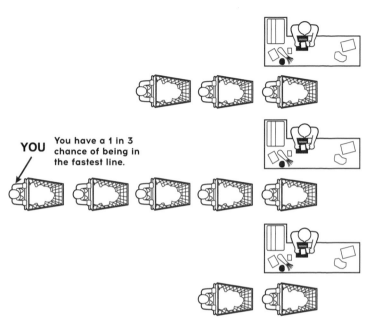

You have a 1 in 3 chance of being in the fastest line.

YOU

QUEUES: THE OTHER ONE IS ALWAYS FASTER

Q

You just want to get up to the checkout till, but all these people are in your way. They don't deserve to get up to the till as much as you do. Waiting is aggravating and worse still is seeing someone who got in line later pass you by. We spend a lot of time waiting around in queues. The research firm Priority Management estimates we spend five years of our lives waiting. That's five years you'll never get back, and you certainly don't want to see someone else passing you up and getting that two minutes of life advantage.

Professor Richard C Larson of the Massachusetts Institute of Technology teaches a seminar on 'queuing theory' and the 'psychology of lines'. He believes shops should always have one long queue instead of several short ones. With short queues you have what he calls 'slips and skips'. The slips happen when somebody moves ahead of you. Skips are when you move ahead of them.

We are thrilled when we get to skip ahead, but the pleasure is outweighed by the disgust at slipping. 'When somebody slips by you, your psychological cost is high,' he told the *Washington Post*. 'You're going to remember that.' If you think this is just a case of negative thinking – think again. Chances are, the queue next to you really will finish first. Let's say you are at the supermarket and there are five lanes open. It's true that, on average, the queues will move at more or less the same rate over time. One will be going faster and then the coupon clipper of the year will bog things down. Another will be cruising along at record speed until the cashier shouts 'Price check!' All in all, they tend to average out, but that probably won't help you much. It comes down to simple odds. Of the five queues, only one can be the speediest.

Therefore, you have only a one in five chance of getting into it. Even if you just consider the lanes to either side of you, you have only a one-in-three chance of being in the fastest. More often than not, then, the other guy will be asked 'Cash or card?' before you.

One other fact to keep in mind when queuing – let's say you are at the post office to renew your vehicle tax along with half of the people in the country. As you wait in line, you get more and more impatient and aggravated. When you get to the front of the queue you snap, 'I've been queuing for an hour!' The cashier snaps back at you, 'No you haven't, this queue is only 15 minutes long!' Guess what? You're both wrong. A classic 1989 study 'Misperceptions of Time in Sales Transactions', published in *Advances in Consumer Research* found that 77 per cent of customers overestimate the amount of time they spend waiting, and 84 per cent of employees underestimate it.

ROAD RAGE ▶ RUSTLING WRAPPERS

ROAD RAGE
AND ROAD RUDENESS

See also *Car Park Battles, Slow Drivers in the Fast Lane.*

By day he is a mild-mannered accountant, well liked by all. Get him behind the wheel and it's a different story. He rides your bumper like one of the villains from *Fast and Furious*. He nearly runs you off the road and pulls into your lane with only millimetres to spare. As he passes he flashes you a one-finger salute. You half expect to see him release an oil slick as he speeds away. You could laugh it all off, but you're behind the wheel, too. Visions of shooting him off the road with laser death rays dance through your head.

Something about driving brings out the worst in people. One study of driving behaviour by a Michigan firm showed that almost 80 per cent of American drivers are angry most of the time while driving. Drivers said their blood boiled at everything from looking for a parking space to having to merge when a highway narrows. The majority of respondents to a 2002 survey by the US National Highway Traffic Safety Administration said they had at some time in the previous year felt threatened by the behaviour of other drivers. In a 2005 telephone survey conducted by ABC and the *Washington Post*, respondents rated road rage as the greatest traffic danger three times more often than any other item on the list, including drink driving. So we think it is a big problem. Is it? It's hard to quantify. Accident statistics only reveal what happened; they don't show the state of mind of the drivers involved. All the American Automobile Association could report with certainty is that 'actions typically associated with aggressive driving' were reported in 56 per cent of fatal crashes from 2003 to 2007.

Researchers at Trinity College Dublin in Ireland chalk it up to 'de-individualization'. That is, people see the traffic offender as a vehicle rather than as a person. Psychologists Leon James and Diane Nahl have spent two decades studying aggressive driving. 'You're protected in your vehicle,' Nahl said. 'There's a sense of isolation – the metal dome

R

around you and the power of the engine. It gives you a false sense of security that you can basically do whatever you want without risk.'

Here is something you probably did not know: the driver of that minivan with the family member stickers on the back window is as likely to flip out on you as the driver with the go-faster stripes stuck on his hot hatch. A Colorado State University study found that drivers who personalize their vehicles with bumper stickers, vanity plates and dashboard bobble heads are more likely to lash out than others. It doesn't matter whether it's a sticker declaring 'Imagine World Peace' or truck nuts dangling from the rear bumper. To the research team, these are all 'territorial markings', and people who like to display them are more aggressive on the road.

The term 'road rage' was coined in England, but the concept is not new. Researchers have uncovered accounts of 'buggy rage' and they suspect there was probably 'chariot rage' as well. Human nature being what it is, road rage will probably not disappear until cars start driving themselves. In the meantime, be careful out there.

R

RUSTLING SWEET WRAPPERS AT THE CINEMA

See also *Coughing in the Theatre*.

You are watching a film – or trying to. The actors are speaking in hushed voices. 'But if we set the fuse . . .' This is when the guy next to you decides it's time to open a wrapped sweet. Crinkle, crackle. 'What about the alarm on the . . .' crinkle, crackle. 'The most important thing is . . .' crinkle, crinkle, crackle, crink. This is when you stand up and shout, 'Will you stop that?!' A large usher personally escorts you out of the cinema.

Whether you're trying to enjoy the show next to a snacking audience member or you're the snacking culprit trying in vain to unwrap a sweet without attracting attention, those rustling wrappers are irritating. Fortunately, a pair of scientists has devoted considerable mental energy to answering the question: 'Is there a way to open a plastic wrapper in a cinema so that it makes less noise?' Unfortunately, the answer to that question is 'no'.

It was a fortuitous accident that turned Eric Kramer of Simon's Rock College in Great Barrington, Massachusetts, and Alexander Lobkovsky of the National Institute of Standards and Technology in Gaithersburg, Maryland, into pioneers in the field of annoying sweet wrapper research. They were graduate students at the University of Chicago when they began studying crumpled plastic membranes, hoping that their investigations would yield some positive uses in automobile safety, the efficient design of packaging materials and the properties of two-dimensional polymers.

Kramer and Lobkovsky began by crumpling a sheet of polyester film 30 to 40 times to make permanent creases. They then made high-resolution digital recordings of the sounds that were produced as they uncreased it. They discovered that the physics of sweet wrappers is highly complex. When a flat plastic wrapper is twisted around a sweet, it is permanently changed. The creases – the scientists call them disorder in the curvature of the material – are responsible for the noises you hear.

When you think you are just unwrapping a sweet, you are actually moving the plastic from one stable configuration to another stable configuration. Every time you do this there is a corresponding click. The sound is not continuous. It is made up of pops that last only a thousandth of a second. The loudness of the random pops has nothing to do with the speed at which you twist the wrapper or even the thickness of the material. In other words, no matter how you do it, it's going to make the same amount of noise.

The best expert advice Kramer and Lobkovsky can give is to open the sweet as fast as you can and get it over and done with.

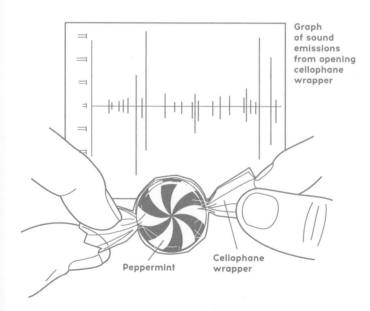

Graph of sound emissions from opening cellophane wrapper

Peppermint

Cellophane wrapper

R

SLOW DRIVERS ▶ STUCK IN TRAFFIC

Speed limit

Fast lane

Speed

SLOW DRIVERS IN THE FAST LANE

See also *Car Park Battles, Road Rage*.

The morning commute is the setting for any number of aggravations – bottle necks, drivers who cut you up only to stop at a pedestrian crossing, trucks that splatter mud all over your windscreen. But what do drivers hate more than anything else? According to Dr Diane Nahl, a psychologist who specializes in our behaviour on the roads, her surveys over two decades of research have revealed that the most aggravating culprit is 'the passive-aggressive driver who's going the speed limit in the fast lane.'

'When someone does that you feel like you're being thwarted,' she says. 'You're being forced to go a speed you don't want to go, and they're in your way. It's a feeling of making people be good and teaching them a lesson. It's all about making sure you're getting what you need and want. If others aren't getting what they need and want that's their problem.'

If you want to get the slow driver out of your way, retired New York state trooper James M Eagan says, the best way is to quickly flash your headlights. 'Do this when you are about three to four truck lengths behind him,' he writes in his book *A Speeder's Guide to Avoiding Tickets: The Essential Manual for Life in the Fast Lane*. If you wait too long, he says, the offending driver may consider you a tailgater and 'punish' you by slowing down or refusing to budge. 'Aggressive drivers want minimum speed limits, not maximum,' wrote traffic psychology researchers Dr Leon James and Dr Diane Nahl in their book *Road Rage and Aggressive Driving*.

'Rushing mania is one of the most common driving obsessions . . . [It] has two complementary elements. One is an extraordinary need to avoid slowing down. The other is the consequent anger against anyone who causes a slow down.'

James believes tailgating is a symptom of a larger problem – a cultural trend to respond to annoyances with anger. 'People feel entitled in public places,' he says. 'If anyone stands in the way I have the right to be angry – maybe retaliate. Take a look at the post office, people stand in line, but what are they thinking? We've had students write down their thoughts and feelings and we get an idea that people carry on, cognitively, a constant verbal attack and criticism of others.'

In any case, tailgating won't get you there any faster. Tailgaters actually get blocked in more often than other drivers because they can't anticipate problems ahead and select the best lane.

SLOW WI-FI

See also *Buffering*.

The experts say slow wi-fi can be blamed on a number of factors, including the fact that you have walls in your house. It's true: the design and technology website Gizmodo maintains that 'walls, floor, furniture, mirrors and metal objects all have a detrimental effect on the signal' and offers the simple suggestion that repositioning your router can work wonders. Simpler than knocking walls down, certainly. The more state-of-the-art your equipment is, the faster it will work and the better it will deal with long distances, they say, and for those who have nothing better to do with their time, there is also the option of nagging your Internet Service Provider to ensure that you are getting what you pay for.

More drastic even than knocking down the walls: unless you are in London or a few other privileged places such as Winchester, you will get a faster connection if you move house. Central London postcodes can expect up to 200 Mb with fibre-optic broadband, whereas locations as diverse as Folkestone, the Wirral and the NEC in Birmingham max out at 76. But, never mind the postcode lottery, it seems that we are all at risk of losing our Internet connection to Russian spies, sharks or fishing fleets.

Some 800,000km (500,000 miles) of cables lie beneath our oceans, placed there by telecommunications companies and, latterly, the likes of Google and Microsoft. The first allowed Queen Victoria to telegraph US President Buchanan in the 1850s; the more recent ones enable most of us to be online 24/7, streaming Netflix and WhatsApping photos of our holidays in the Seychelles to disgruntled relatives at home.

Although some of these cables lie as deep as 9,000m (29,530ft) below the surface of the ocean and are carefully arranged to avoid coral reefs, shipwrecks and other hazards, they are not immune to accident or even sabotage (that, according to a 2015 *New York Times* report, is where the threat from Russian spies comes in). The sharks aren't a

S

shock-horror story, either – a 2009 report commissioned by the United Nations Environment Programme and the International Cable Protection Committee reported that in the Canary Islands as early as 1989 'the first deep-ocean fibre-optic cable failed on four occasions as a result of shark attacks in water depths of 1,060–1,900m [3,478–6,233ft]'. The fact that at least one of these predators carelessly left some of its teeth behind has enabled experts to identify it as a crocodile shark (Pseudocarcharias kamoharai), at a mere metre long decidedly petite by shark standards. Imagine what a 6-m (20-ft) great white, with its thousands of serrated teeth, could do. Recently, the various consortia have been coating their cables in stronger and stronger synthetic fibres, but the sharks – possibly attracted by electromagnetic signals in the cables – continue their attacks.

Ships' anchors can sever cables, too – they did it twice in the space of a month off the coast of Kenya in February 2012, affecting communications between East Africa, the Middle East and Western Europe. It can happen anywhere, any time. Consider that before you go to the trouble of moving to Winchester.

S

SNORING

He snores, you say. That doesn't really begin to describe it. Your bed partner's nose produces a rumbling that frightens small children . . . in the next time zone. A long, fierce vibration followed by a teasing pause and a tense wait. You know another snort is coming.

Sari Zayed of Davis, California, made headlines a couple of decades ago when a city noise enforcement officer issued her with a $50 fine at 1:30 in the morning after a neighbour complained her snoring kept him awake at night. Zayed got the last laugh. She sued for $24,500 for stress, lost wages and emotional strain, and settled out of court for $13,500. Snorers aren't trying to keep others awake at night. Most of the time, they don't even know they snore – they are, after all, unconscious at the time. Some anthropologists have suggested that snoring is a primitive way of keeping beasts away at night. Ear, nose and throat doctors take a different view.

When you breathe, you create a negative pressure to suck in air. When you sleep, the soft tissues in the back of your mouth and throat – the soft palate, tonsils, adenoids and uvula (that little thing that hangs down) – relax and prevent air from flowing freely. You reflexively try to pull in air quickly, creating turbulence.

Estimates of the number of snorers in the United States range from 80 to 90 million. The tendency to snore increases with age. While only 30 per cent of young people snore, 40 per cent of those over 40 do. Otolaryngologist Kent Wilson of the University of Minnesota at Minneapolis hung a microphone over 1,139 people as they slept and found that some snores topped 55 decibels, about the volume of rush-hour traffic. Want to know if you are one of them? There are now snore tracking apps for that. Doctors take snoring seriously. The most serious form is sleep apnoea, in which the sleeper actually stops breathing for periods of at least 10 seconds, hundreds of times a night. During as much as half their sleep time, patients with sleep apnoea may show below-average concentrations of oxygen in their blood. A lack of oxygen

S

Uvula

ZZZZZzzz   zzZZZZZ

The sound
of snoring
can exceed
55 decibels.

can cause the heart to pump harder and, over time, can contribute to high blood pressure.

During REM sleep, the brain sends out an inhibitor that basically paralyses the body, presumably to keep you from acting out vivid dreams. When a sleep apnoea sufferer's breathing is cut off, the body rouses itself with a jolt of adrenaline. Breathing resumes, the person falls back to sleep, and the whole thing starts again. These 'micro-arousals' can happen as many as six hundred times a night, disrupting a snorer's sleep cycle. Studies have linked apnoea-induced sleepiness to an increase in car accidents. A study by the Mayo Clinic also shows that spouses of heavy snorers lose an average of one hour's sleep a night.

People have tried to develop snoring cures as far back as the American Revolution when soldiers sewed small cannonballs into pockets on the back of the snoring-offenders' uniforms so they would not roll onto their backs. Today, more than three hundred anti-snoring devices are registered with the US Patent and Trademark Office.

To reduce your night-time noise making, doctors suggest losing weight, avoiding alcohol within three hours before you go to sleep, not sleeping on your back (some suggest attaching something bulky like a tennis ball to the inside of the back of your pyjamas) and, ironically, getting enough sleep. If that doesn't work, consult a doctor. There are a number of things they can try, such as breathing masks, mouthpieces and surgery.

An international research project conducted by the Human Sleep Research Laboratory at the Stanford Research Institute in the United States and Ludwig-Maximilians-Universität in Munich, Germany, has taken a different approach. They don't want to know how to stop snoring, they want to know whether people's irritation with snoring has to do with the type of snore or the type of listener. They played a sample from '550 representative snoring sequences' to subjects who rated their level of annoyance on a scale from 0 to 100. They concluded that 'the listeners' noise sensitivity is at least equally relevant for the snoring annoyance as the snoring sound itself'.

S

SOME ASSEMBLY REQUIRED: FLAT-PACK FURNITURE

S

When you walked through the clean, stylish Swedish furniture store, you imagined yourself living in the perfectly decorated mini-rooms with pleasure and optimism. Then you take home a box of wooden slats, metal bolts and a diagram. Your future begins to seem much less rosy very fast. If figuring out how to get part A into slot B has driven you to utter choice four-letter words, throw things around the room or even threatened to derail your marriage, you are not alone.

It seems that IKEA-related complaints come up frequently in couples counselling. 'Couples tend to extrapolate from the small conflicts that arise while shopping for and building furniture that perhaps they aren't so made for one another after all,' Maisie Chou Chaffin, a London-based clinical psychologist told the *Atlantic*.

There are real gender differences, and gendered cultural expectations, about the assembly of furniture. After Norway's prime minister accused IKEA of sexism for showing only men in its instruction manuals, the company responded by adding more women and arguing that, in fact, women were better at assembling their products than men were. Petra Hesser, who was then the head of IKEA's Germany division said: 'A woman will neatly lay out all the screws while a man will throw them in a pile. Something always goes missing.'

So researchers set out to test the hypothesis and found: 1) There is something to Hesser's description of how men and women approach 'some assembly required' tasks; and 2) her conclusion that women do a better job was entirely wrong. A Norwegian research team asked 40 men and 40 women in their twenties to assemble a kitchen trolley. Some people got the instructions, others only received a drawing of what the end product should look like. When they had the instructions, men and women took the same amount of time (about 23 minutes) to put the thing together, and both had equally impressive, or unimpressive, results.

Of those who had to figure things out from a drawing, there was a 20 per cent difference between men and women in terms of how long it took to complete the task. The women also assembled more faulty trolleys with missing shelves or railings. In all, men with no instructions did about as well as the men with the instructions, finishing only a minute slower and not making enough mistakes to make the difference statistically meaningful. So Hesser was right: women do take a more systematic approach, because they need to. Men's habit of throwing the instructions aside can be a source of frustration and argument.

Studies have long identified differences in spatial ability between men and women. The science is still out, however, as to whether this is the result of nature or nurture. In a recent study, researchers had subjects from two genetically similar but culturally distinct peoples in north-east India complete a visual puzzle. Women from the patriarchal culture performed more slowly than the men. In the culture where women ruled, there were no gender differences in performance. In another study, women were asked to imagine that they were men when doing a mental rotation test. When they did, they performed just as well as the men did. They also did better when they were told ahead of time that women usually outperformed the men. So women's slower times and reliance on instructions might be the result of conditioning and a lack of confidence.

Of course, individual results vary, and not every man who thinks he can do a great job without the instructions actually can. As writer Jon Tevlin said, 'I know from personal experience that using only pictures of men assembling IKEA furniture can lead some to believe . . . that men actually CAN assemble IKEA furniture.'

The expectation that every man should be able to assemble items like furniture often creates conflict and it doesn't take a lot of tension to drive a wedge between a couple. In a 2014 study, researchers at Monmouth University, New Jersey and Ursinus College, Pennsylvania studied the effect of frustration on romantic feelings. They split 120 subjects into two groups. One group was given the simple, stress-free task of writing down numbers chronologically; the other group received a set of difficult maths problems. When they had finished both groups were asked to make a list of compliments about their partner. The stressed group identified 15 per cent fewer admirable traits in their beloveds.

The main way to avoid furniture assembly frustration, say the experts, is to go easy on yourself and allow plenty of time to get the job done. Walk away and come back if you have to. If that doesn't work, maybe you need to buy pre-assembled furniture. No one wants to have a half-assembled wardrobe listed as an asset in a divorce proceeding.

S

SONG STUCK IN YOUR HEAD, OR CEREBRUM-ANNOYING REFLUX ACTION

E veryone has had the experience of having an annoyingly catchy, and often hated, song lodged firmly in the mind. The Germans use the word *Ohrwurm*, which translates as 'earworm' or 'earwig', for tunes that invade the consciousness.

The scientific literature records a few extreme cases. Dr Judith Rapoport, who specializes in treating victims of obsessive compulsive disorder, treated a man who heard the same six fiddle notes for 31 years. 'When he finally admitted it to his wife, she wept with joy because she had thought that he just wasn't interested in listening to her,' she said. In 2000 an American man had surgery of the right lateral temporal cortex to stop the song 'Owner of a Lonely Heart' by Yes from playing over and over in his mind.

Not even animals are immune. A group of scientists at the University of Sydney in Australia studied a humpback whale song from 1995 to 1998. They found that a song that was at first sung only by two males quickly spread. By the end of 1997 the entire group had adopted it.

There is, apparently, some kind of neurological underpinning in all this. Songs can be triggered by stimulating an area in the brain that processes sound patterns. When the first edition of this book came out in 2001, researchers had not devoted a great deal of serious study to earworms, but they are now working hard to fill the knowledge gap.

A 2016 study by the American Psychological Association identified the types of songs that are most apt to get lodged in the grey matter. They are usually up-tempo with easily remembered melodies and more repetition than the average pop song. The researchers collected data from 3,000 people over three years and published their results in the journal *Psychology of Aesthetics, Creativity, and the Arts*. They compiled a list of the most common offenders. Number one was Lady Gaga's 'Bad Romance', followed by, appropriately enough, Kylie Minogue's 'Can't Get You Out of My Head'. That same year OnePoll did a survey of

S

S

songs that are hardest to shake for the *Sun*. They found that the Proclaimers' 'I'm Gonna Be (500 Miles)' was the catchiest song in the universe. The UK list was topped by mostly older songs like Bon Jovi's 'Living on a Prayer' and the Village People's 'YMCA' as well as the theme songs from *Benny Hill, Friends* and *Star Wars*. This caused the authors to speculate that music today is not as catchy as it used to be. Whereas the US study's top ten was Lady Gaga heavy, suggesting that the age of the songs was the result of different methodology, not the inherent melodic qualities of different decades. (Queen's 'Bohemian Rhapsody' and Journey's 'Don't Stop Believing' spread their tentacles into brains on both sides of the Atlantic.) The 1943 novelty song 'Mairzy Dotes' is surely as hooky as the 1960s 'Monkees Theme', the 1980s 'Karma Chameleon', the 2000s 'Who Let the Dogs Out', or the 2014 hit 'Uptown Funk'. Open surveys tend to find about three-quarters of people report unique songs not experienced by others.

But the real question is not what music gets stuck, it is how to get rid of a song that does. The only way to dislodge it, say researchers, is to distract yourself. Try solving a tricky anagram or doing a crossword puzzle. Being 'cognitively engaged' can force the intrusive melody out of your active memory. The trick is to come up with something that is challenging, but not too challenging. If a problem is too hard, your brain will give up, allowing space for your brain to 'do the "Time Warp" again'.

S

HOW MILK BECOMES SOUR

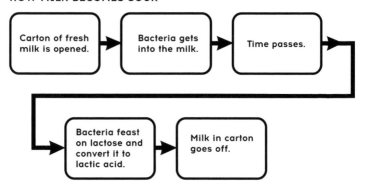

Carton of fresh milk is opened.	Bacteria gets into the milk.	Time passes.

Bacteria feast on lactose and convert it to lactic acid.	Milk in carton goes off.

SOUR MILK

Nothing spoils your morning like casually pouring milk on your cereal and taking a big mouthful only to discover – eeewwww – the milk is off.

Sour milk is fermented milk. Milk is made up of fat, proteins and sugars. It is actually between 12 and 13 per cent solid, more solid than many vegetables. The composition of the milk is influenced by the breed and age of the specific cow and when the milk was drawn. The last milk drawn at each milking is richest in fat. The same foodstuffs that are useful to humans are a feast for bacteria.

When the milk comes out of the cow, it is actually bacteria-free. Once the air gets to it, the bacteria begin their colonization. Pasteurization – heating milk to 71.7°C (161°F) for 15 seconds – kills the kinds of bacteria that might result in disease, but a few harmless spoilage bacteria remain behind. As long as the carton or bottle remains unopened, few new bacteria can get into the liquid. Thus, an unopened container lasts longer than one that is opened. The spoilage bacteria do not do well in very low temperatures, which is why milk must be refrigerated. It should be kept at a temperature below 4°C (40°F). At that temperature, it should last about 14 days.

During those two weeks, the spoilage bacteria feast on the milk sugar, or lactose. They convert the lactose into lactic acid through a fermentation process. When there is enough lactic acid, the milk gains that distinctive sour smell and odd taste. Skimmed milk tends to stay fresh longer than whole milk because whole milk has more lactose. If you have any of your grandmother's recipes, you may have a few that call for 'sour milk'. The acid in the sour milk reacts with bicarbonate of soda to create bubbles of carbon dioxide that make baked goods rise.

Such recipes pre-date pasteurization. These days, milk that has had time to go sour probably has had time to attract and grow some unhealthy spoilage bacteria as well. Instead of using sour milk, substitute buttermilk in those recipes for the same effect.

Curdling of milk is caused by protein called casein. It is normally dispersed throughout the fluid of the milk. When the milk has aged as long as it apparently does in your fridge, the curds (solid) separate from the whey (liquid).

As for those 'sell by' dates on milk – milk will not instantly expire on that day. Milk containers are stamped with a date that is 14 days from the time the milk was pasteurized and packed. It takes about two days for milk to get from the cow to the store. There it is refrigerated at 4°C (40°F) or less. It should then last another week past the 'expiration date', assuming you also keep it refrigerated.

S

SPEEDING TICKETS

See also *Road Rage, Slow Drivers in the Fast Lane.*

L ittle can dampen your mood as quickly as watching the police car you zoomed past pull out and turn on the blue lights. Then there's the question: 'Do you know how fast you were going?' Is there a right answer to that question? If you say, 'Yes, I was going 85,' you admit you were speeding. If you say, 'I was going the speed limit,' you annoy the officer because you both know that's a lie. If you want to avoid getting a ticket, James M Eagan, a retired New York state trooper and author of the book *A Speeder's Guide to Avoiding Tickets*, suggests you put the ball back in the police officer's court. 'Your best bet is to try a comment like, "I just wasn't paying attention like I should have, officer. How fast was I going?"'

Most of us are more likely to talk ourselves into tickets than out of them. To increase your chances of driving off with a warning, Eagan says you should always try to reduce the police officer's fear and feed his (or her) ego. Try to engage him in conversation so he sees you as a human being and don't do anything to challenge his authority.

The problem is that everything about a speeding stop is calculated to increase your fear and deflate your ego. A study by the Canadian Mounties has shown that if the officer is wearing mirrored sunglasses your feelings of stress and fear rise. You are likely to perceive the officer as more aggressive and less courteous than if you could see his eyes. If he is wearing a visible holstered gun, your anger and fear rise even more. Frightened, angry drivers are more likely to mouth off. If you want to avoid that ticket, it is your job to break the vicious cycle. Don't apologize or promise not to speed again, Eagan says – the officer lives in the same world as the rest of us and he knows just about everyone speeds. He doesn't believe you are sorry, and he doesn't believe you won't do it again.

'The members of the hierarchy do not want you to slow down,' he writes. 'Despite their public service announcements to the contrary,

S

Mirrored sunglasses increase driver feeling of stress and fear.

Intimidated driver is likely to lash out.

S

they want you to speed so you can get a ticket.' And yes, there is data to back him up. In 2009 an article in the *Journal of Law and Economics* revealed that two separate studies had found a small but statistically significant correlation between a drop in local government revenue and an increase in traffic fines. The bad news is, they found that, once ticketing increases, it does not go back down when the council becomes more flush.

If you do get a ticket, you might try what University of California physicist Dmitri Krioukov did when he was charged with making a rolling stop at a stop sign. He wrote a paper called 'The Proof of Innocence', complete with graphs and formulas. It explained, 'If a car stops at a stop sign, an observer, e.g. a police officer, located at a certain distance perpendicular to the car trajectory, must have an illusion that the car does not stop, if the following three conditions are satisfied: (1) The observer measures not the linear but angular speed of the car; (2) The car decelerates and subsequently accelerates relatively fast; and (3) There is a short-time obstruction of the observer's view of the car by an external object, e.g., another car, at the moment when both cars are near the stop sign.' In English, 'I did stop – you just didn't see it right.' That is to say, again as Krioukov put it: the police officer was not lying; it was just that his 'perception of reality did not properly reflect reality'. This worked for Krioukov. Your results may vary.

S

SPOILERS

See also *Buffering*.

You had a late meeting last night so you recorded the final episode of a series you have been watching obsessively. You went to bed imagining how much you would enjoy the big TV moment. In the morning you make your coffee (and spill some of it after eight steps), you pick up your smartphone to check in with your friends and the first status update is how surprised your best friend was by the way the producers killed off your favourite character. You curse your best friend.

There are more ways than ever now for plots to be spoiled, which leads to another annoyance, constant 'spoiler alerts'. In the old days, before recording devices, the only way to give a story away was to go to the cinema or read a book first and then blurt the story out in person. It did happen, however, and it was annoying. An example from my youth (when we had Betamax tapes) was when our English teacher assigned us Harper Lee's *To Kill a Mockingbird*. **Warning: this anecdote contains spoilers.** We had a suitable period of time in which to read the book, but one enterprising student ploughed through it in one night. The teacher asked him, 'Were you surprised when Boo Radley saved Jem and Scout?' The entire classroom groaned.

Promoters can spoil a film or television show before it is even

S

released by including too much information in the trailer. Studios don't wait around long to see if a film is a hit or a bomb. If it doesn't do big box office numbers the first weekend, it's headed straight to a streaming service. So they start promoting the films earlier and earlier with thrill ride trailers. They're called 'trailers' by the way, because in the old days they used to play them after the feature film. Now they're up front where there is more of a captive audience. Some critics say the tell-all previews are part of a Hollywood trend away from subtlety. The studios, the argument goes, believe you won't go to a film unless everything is spelled out for you.

'Today, if I had to cut the trailer for *Citizen Kane*, they would probably make me explain what Rosebud is,' said one editor. 'But by that point they'd probably have changed Rosebud to Jen because the name Rosebud didn't test well among women 18 to 34.'

Here is the twist: the studio is probably right. We complain a lot about spoilers, but the only study done on them to date found that knowing the ending of a story in advance actually enhanced readers' enjoyment. Nicholas Christenfeld and Jonathan Leavitt, researchers from the University of California at San Diego, had subjects read 12 short stories. There were mysteries, literary stories and stories with ironic plot twists. For some of the subjects, the ending was revealed in introductory text before the story began ('In this classic story in which the butler did it,' for example.) The others did not have a similar introduction. Then they asked the readers how much they enjoyed the story. In every case, the readers with the spoiled versions enjoyed them more. They hypothesize that knowing the ending in advance allows readers to focus on the details and not be distracted by wondering how it is going to turn out.

Of course, the readers in the study were given stories they were not already invested in. They had no previous expectations of how much they would enjoy the story. When you're a *Star Wars* fan waiting for the next instalment, or you're obsessed with *Game of Thrones* or binge-watching old episodes of *Downton Abbey*, much of the pleasure comes from imagining how you will feel as the next episode unfolds and your

S

characters go on new adventures. 'An unwanted spoiler does take something away,' wrote *Time* magazine's TV critic James Poniewozik, 'but not, I think, the pleasure of actually reading or watching a story. Rather, it takes away from the anticipation before watching it – wondering who dies, whether they'll get off the island.' So science be damned. I haven't watched the last season of *Orange Is the New Black* yet. Don't give the plot away.

S

People need more
personal space
behind them.

Personal
space

Size of the egg-shaped
zone varies according
to how well we know
the person or people.

S

STANDING TOO CLOSE

See also *Aeroplane Legroom, Armrest Wars, Inefficient Pavement Pass, Too Much Perfume.*

You are in a public place and a strange woman comes up to you and engages you in conversation. As she speaks, you become nervous and stiff. She is standing about a step closer than you want her to be. You try to back away without being obvious, and a strange dance begins. During the course of the conversation you move halfway across the room, but she always ends up just a little bit closer than you want her to be. By all accounts, she is trying to be pleasant and social, and yet you can't wait for her to go away. Why? She has invaded your personal space.

According to American anthropologist Edward T Hall, a pioneering researcher in the field of proxemics – the study of our use of space – we set our boundaries by the time we reach the age of 12. Different cultures have different boundaries, but no culture is without its own sense of space. Every person, indeed, every animal, is surrounded by an invisible egg-shaped field. The reason it is not a circle is that we will let people come in closer from the front than from behind.

Hall described four distinctive spatial zones. The closest extends outwards about 46cm (18in). Only those who are the most intimate, lovers or parents with children, are allowed within the boundary. The next zone, reserved for close friends, extends from 46cm to 1.2m (18in to 4ft). Co-workers and casual acquaintances are expected to remain at a distance of 1.2 to 3m (4 to 10ft). Strangers are permitted from 3 to 7.6m (10 to 25ft). When we encounter people with a different sense of personal space, such as people who were raised in different cultures, it makes us uncomfortable, irritable and, in extreme cases, physically ill.

When most people lived in rural areas or on farms, personal space was not a pressing issue. It has been estimated that in medieval times the average person saw one hundred other people in the course of a lifetime. As the Industrial Revolution swept the world and crowded

S

people into cities, we developed a variety of methods of coping with the constant infringement on our space. We have a set of unwritten rules about how close to stand and when to acknowledge others. We create boundaries by placing coats or books on the seat beside us. In elevators, we face forwards and rarely make eye contact. Even though no one taught you in so many words, as a Northern European or North American, you know that you can ignore a person standing 3m (10ft) away but, once they get to about 2m (8ft), it is time to smile or say hello.

When space is limited, we try to preserve an internal sense of space by shutting ourselves off from others. If we cannot get the people out of our space, we do our best to pretend they are not people. This is easily observed in commuter trains, buses and planes. The legal capacity of a New York subway train allows 0.5 cubic metres (20 cubic feet) of space per person, but the passengers have to stand or sit closer to each other when using handrails. The Tokyo subway crowds passengers into 0.1 cubic metres (5 cubic feet) or less.

Passengers try to create their own space by reading books or magazines or looking out the window. If they can't, they will often look down towards their feet and generally avoid eye contact with the people in the surrounding seats. The exercise is stressful and exhausting. Researchers have found that after an hour's ride on a crowded Japanese commuter train, it takes about an hour and a half for a commuter to completely get over the strain and fatigue.

Robert Sommer, a psychologist at the University of California at Davis, wrote an entire book, *Personal Space,* on how people react when we break such rules. He conducted his research by going into libraries and sitting too close to people.

'They begin by tapping their toes,' he says. 'They pull at their hair. They get completely rigid. It may not trigger a full-blown schizophrenic episode, but it's clearly not good for your health.'

Furrowed brow

Hands clamped to steering wheel

Commuters have higher blood pressure and higher rates of calling in sick.

STUCK IN TRAFFIC

See also *Road Rage*.

'I just want to get there! Just let me get there! I just want to get off this road!'

By the time we get to work, our blood pressure is up, we are too tired and irritated to function well, and we are more easily frustrated. A 2016 report from research group TRIP determined that, while the United States' interstate highway system has only about 2.5 per cent of the miles of lanes nationwide, it carries 25 per cent of traffic. Since 2000, traffic has grown at twice the rate of the construction of new lanes. The Texas A&M Transportation Institute, meanwhile, determined that US commuters lose an average of 42 hours per year to traffic delays. If you have the misfortune of travelling on one of the nation's ten most gridlocked roads, the number doubles to 84 hours. That's three-and-a-half days per year of sitting in traffic jams. And no, no one likes that.

Rush-hour traffic is largely an urban problem, so it is no surprise that New York invented 'gridlock'. The term came into common use

S

during a transport workers' strike in 1980. It sent so many commuters out in their cars that Manhattan's street grid was paralysed – locked. For one car to move one car length in downtown Manhattan, one car had to exit the island uptown.

Raymond Novaco, a professor of psychology at the University of California at Irvine, studies the negative effects of commuting. 'Regardless of age, income, race or social position, red lights and crowded freeways make us frustrated,' Novaco told *Prevention* magazine. 'We found that the longer the commute, the higher the blood pressure.' Novaco's team also found that those with long commutes had more work absences due to colds or flu. Plus, long commutes create more pollution, which contributes to all our respiratory distress. About 40 per cent of smog is due to exhaust emissions.

None of this is all that surprising, but did you know that there is a correlation between long commutes and divorce? Researchers at Umeå University in Sweden studied couples and found that when one partner's commute was more than 45 minutes they were 40 per cent more likely to get divorced. The scholars blamed stress and anxiety for the conflicts. The silver lining is that, if you manage to stick it out for five years, the divorce rate for commuters falls to only 1 per cent higher than that of homebodies.

If you want a happy life, you are better off taking a job that pays less and has a short commute, says a team from the University of Basel in Switzerland. They found that the aggravation of having a long commute outweighed any happiness a higher salary might bring.

Is there anything you can do to make a commute better? Science suggests the answer might be a slow jam. Stephen Fairclough, a professor of psychophysiology at Liverpool John Moores University in England, had subjects drive a course in a simulator and frustrated their attempts to arrive at their destination on time with virtual traffic. The background music in the car had an impact on their stress levels. Fairclough found that the people who listened to no music or to high-tempo 'aggressive music' had elevated blood pressure. Those who listened to soothing or sad music, what he described as 'low activation', did not.

TEEN ANGST ▶ TROLLS

TEEN ANGST

'You're ruining my life!'

The teen years are inevitably a time of angst, arguments and utter turmoil, right? Not so fast. There is no reason it has to be that way. In fact, it may be our belief that the teen years are a time of angst that causes us to experience it. So don't begin with the idea that you are in for a bumpy ride. Lots of parents get along great with their teens, and their children are generally happy and well adjusted.

Don't believe me? Ask the psychologists. Most studies indicate that only about 20 per cent of adolescents undergo pronounced turmoil and the ones that do are for the most part adolescents with clear-cut psychological problems or who come from disrupted family backgrounds.

The idea that your teen is one step away from becoming a juvenile delinquent and will hate you from ages 12 to 17 is thoroughly Western. In Japan and China, where they do not have such an expectation, the teenage years usually pass without incident. In Japan, 80 to 90 per cent of teens describe their home lives as 'fun' or 'pleasant' and report positive relations with their parents. The same can be said of families in India, sub-Saharan Africa, South-East Asia and much of the Arab world. This doesn't mean that you should move to Tanzania for the sake of family harmony. The point here is that there is nothing inevitable about the growing pains of this age.

One theory as to why Western cultures report more angst (besides our insistence on looking for it) is that in most non-Western cultures, teenagers are treated more like maturing adults and given adult responsibilities. In the West, where we see the teen years as an extension of childhood and expect young people to be nurtured and protected, they may be more likely to rebel against parental restrictions.

A common mistake among parents of teenagers, according to Anthony E Wolf, a clinical psychologist and the author of many books on parenting adolescents, is to assume the role of wise teacher and to try to dispense a lifetime of knowledge at every opportunity. One reason your teenager may appear to become sullen and withdrawn could be that you are not actually listening to him when he speaks. You may think that you are, but pay close attention to your side of the conversation. Does it go like this?

Your teenager says, 'This guy in my class came out as gay the other day.'

'You know there is nothing wrong with being gay, right? You know your father and I would always love you even if you were gay.'

'Whoah, Mum. I was just talking about something that happened in school.' This is when the teenager stops talking.

By lecturing instead of listening you have shut your child down. Wolf's advice on having a good relationship with your teenagers? 'Shut up.' If you genuinely feel you must comment, the best strategy is to wait until a separate time, or at least until the conversation tapers off.

The belief that the teen years are bound to be full of stress can actually cause problems. It might lead you to dismiss a real problem as a 'passing phase' or a normal part of growing up. If you continue to have good communication with your kids during the teen years, you will be better equipped to recognize the signs of real problems like clinical depression if they do arise.

TELEMARKETING

The phone rings in the middle of dinner. 'Hello?' A moment passes. You hear a cacophony of voices in the background. 'Hello?' You repeat. 'Hello, Mr Smith, I'm calling regarding your credit card. Because you are such a valued customer . . .' No one knows exactly who first had the idea to pick up a phone and start selling. It simply evolved as a logical next step from the door-to-door salesman.

A 1927 telephone sales manual published by the Bell Telephone Company of Pennsylvania touted the potential of the technology for sales: 'The telephone provides the simplest, most effective and most economical means of increasing the number of contacts between salesman and buyer.' In the early days, however, the phone was used mostly to set up in-person sales meetings. An early example of the phrase 'Your call is important to us' is associated with in-person meetings in a 1964 notice from an Indiana newspaper: 'McGill Manufacturing has an interesting and most helpful fold-over brochure . . . Inside the fold under the words "your call is important to us" is a wealth of information on the best times to call on executives . . .'

Telemarketing as we know it today really took off in the late 1970s and early 1980s. In the decades that followed, technology revolutionized the annoying art. Thanks to computer technology, telemarketing has become highly efficient and highly profitable. Most telemarketing organizations now use predictive dialling systems. With predictive dialling, a computer places the call. If the line is busy or if no one picks up, it dials another number. If you do pick up, it connects the call to an operator. This is why you often hear a telltale delay when you pick up the phone. (The good news is, it does give you an opportunity to hang up. If there is a delay accented by the sound of many other people talking in the background, there's good chance it's not a personal call.)

If it seems you have been getting more hang-up calls than in the past, you can blame this on predictive dialling as well. The computers dial numbers even when all the operators are busy. With busy signals and non-answers, odds are that at least one operator will have completed a call (or had someone slam the phone down) by the time the machine connects. Sometimes, though, the computer dials a number, you pick up, and there are no operators available. The machine hangs up on you.

Phone call, probably from telemarketer

Dinner

Companies can set the percentage of hang-up calls a system allows – this is called the abandonment rate. The higher the rate, the more hang-ups. The Direct Marketing Association recommends an abandonment rate of no higher than 5 per cent, but some telemarketers are setting the rate as high as 40 per cent. They want the phones to be constantly dialling. When operators have to dial manually, they spend only 15 minutes out of an hour selling, according to a spokesperson for EIS International, which makes predictive dialling systems. With the aid of the system, they can increase talk time up to 45 minutes an hour. Productivity has been known to increase by 200 to 300 per cent.

So the marketers love them, but we hate them. We consider such calls an invasion of our privacy and time. In the United States in 2010, it finally seemed as though there was a solution to telemarketing: the federal Do Not Call Registry. The day it opened to the public, its website was visited 1,000 times . . . every second. By the end of the first day, 750,000 numbers had signed up, and for a while it seemed to be working. The Telephone Preference Service offers a similar service in the UK.

Then voice-over Internet protocols made it easy and inexpensive to set up call centres in foreign countries beyond the reach of the authorities. Now all bets are off. We are bombarded with calls trying to sell solar panels, or asking you to claim a cruise you have supposedly won or confusing messages about PPI claims. The US Federal Trade Commission (FTC) received about 3 million complaints in 2015 about nuisance calls.

Certainly we are not on our best behaviour when dealing with telemarketers. We hang up on them. We scream at them and plot revenge against them. Businesses have found that this is especially true when the caller is based in another country and has a pronounced accent. This situation combines annoyance with anger at outsourcing.

Technology has come up with a solution to this problem as well. This author recently picked up the phone to be greeted by an overly cheery woman with an all-American Midwestern accent. There was something about the call that made me suspect she was not entirely human. 'Are you a robot?' I asked. 'No, I am a human being,' she said, again in a way that was less than convincing. After this she began to say two things at once, and I was treated to a surreal overlapping cacophony of a sales pitch combined with an assurance that I was speaking to a real, live human being.

What happened in this case was that I was, in fact, speaking to a person, but the person was not speaking to me. They call it 'voice conversion' or 'agent-assisted automation technology'. When I spoke, an agent in the Philippines or India responded by performing keystrokes or clicking on a screen to play back pre-recorded responses. This eliminates regional accents and ensures that agents stay 'on script'. As an added benefit, it reduces some of the stress in the call centre itself, creating a buffer between an irate customer and the person on the other end of the phone. That's when it works well. When it doesn't, someone pushes two buttons at once and the secret is revealed.

In the UK, the Information Commissioner's Office advises on dealing with nuisance calls and enforces regulations on direct marketing companies. It is also possible to block certain numbers on mobiles phones and landlines. Maybe that will do the trick.

TOAST ALWAYS LANDS BUTTER-SIDE DOWN

Toast

Butter

Floor just before weekly cleaning

Why is it that, if you drop a piece of toast, chances are, it will land butter-side down? Some scientists say this is not true. According to the makers of a BBC science programme, *Q.E.D.*, the reason we believe the toast is apt to land on the buttery side is that we remember all the times it lands badly and forget the times it lands well. Physicist Robert Matthews set out to prove them wrong. 'The experiments carried out by the programme were dynamically inappropriate,' he wrote in the *European Journal of Physics*, 'in that they consisted of people simply tossing buttered bread into the air.' Matthews tested his theory by dropping pieces of buttered toast over the side of a table.

When that got 'sort of messy' he switched to toast-sized pieces of wood. He discovered that toast does, in fact, tend to land butter-side down. It has nothing to do with the weight of the butter. It has to do with gravitational torque and the height of the average table.

Once the toast slides off the edge of the plate, it starts to flip, but the gravitation torque is not sufficient enough to right the toast again before it hits the floor. So, if you sense your toast is about to take a tumble, Matthews suggests giving it a swipe with your hand to increase its speed at take-off. If you don't possess the requisite skill to save your bread in this manner, he includes a few more entertaining methods of preventing a butter-side-down mishap, including eating tiny squares of toast, buttering the underside or 'tying the toast to a cat, which of course knows how to get right-side up during a fall'.

TOILET SEAT LEFT UP

See also *Yellow Spots on Public Toilet Seats.*

You stumble into the bathroom in the middle of the night. Half asleep you sit on the toilet, only to find that your cohabitator of the masculine gender has left the seat in the upright position. You receive a rude awakening as you tumble into the bowl. Why can't he just put the blasted thing down when he is finished?

Leaving the toilet seat up is, anecdotally at least, one of the main causes of minor marital spats. An unscientific poll conducted by a blog called UKBathrooms found (perhaps unsurprisingly given its focus) that poor bathroom habits were the leading cause of bickering and that it was the position of the loo seat that caused 48 per cent of those tiffs. Whether or not couples actually argue a great deal about this issue, we certainly believe they do.

So what is the rule? Is he lazy and rude when he leaves it up or is the problem your assumption that toilet seat positioning is a man's job? Fortunately, an enterprising Michigan State University economist, Jay Pil Choi, used statistics to come up with a definitive answer. The equation he employed (you can find it at https://msu.edu/~choijay/etiquette.pdf) is beyond my mathematical capacity.

The underlying reasoning is this. You begin with a household shared by men and women. Women always sit on the porcelain fixture. Men sometimes sit, but they also sometimes stand. To quote a famous children's book, everyone poops. If you leave the seat up, then, either a man or a woman might have to reposition it depending on the particular call of nature. So, on the surface it seems that it is most efficient, and less likely to put anyone out if it is left down and only lifted when needed. Problem solved. But wait! We're only scratching the surface.

It seems we do not defecate and urinate in equal proportion. If you are average, you poo once a day and pee seven times. (There are detailed graphs on this in the article if you want to see them.) So the question of whether the seat should be left up or down actually varies depending on the number of standers and sitters in the household. In a house where the number of women is equal to or greater than the number of men, then the rule should be seat down. To leave it up, men need to outnumber women by a certain ratio to 'minimize the aggregate costs of inconvenience'.

T

FANTASTIC MOVIES TONIGHT!

DON'T MISS THESE EITHER!!

TOO MANY STREAMING SERVICES

See also *Slow Wi-Fi.*

Y ou have had a hard day at work and you are ready to sit on the sofa and watch a good movie. You fire up Netflix and scan through its listings, and scan, and scan. Why aren't there any new movies? You already binge watched *Orange is the New Black.* So you subscribe to Amazon Prime Instant Video and Now TV or Sky Go. With all that you're spending why can't you just have one source for your entertainment?

There was a time when you could walk into the video rental shop and walk out with just about any film or show (assuming it had not already been checked out). You did not have to drive to six shops. Of course, this had its drawbacks. You had to leave your house and you had to return the videos on time or risk late fees. Leaving the house is not that popular, so when American company Netflix came up with the idea of a DVD by mail service, it revolutionized how people rented movies in the United States. Of course, that had its own annoyances. You had to wait for a movie to show up through your letterbox, and by the time it came, you were no longer in the mood to watch it.

We can have endless streaming for £7.49 a month, and yet we are thwarted in our desire to have endless streaming of stuff we actually want to watch at that price. Our favourite films invariably show up on whatever service we're not subscribed to. The satirical site The Onion summed up this state of affairs with two headlines: 'Netflix Instant Thinking about Adding Good Movie' and 'Netflix Introduces New "Browse Endlessly" Plan.'

The experts say this is a state of affairs that is not destined to change any time soon. The reason is something media moguls call 'windowing'. Films go through a cycle with various interested parties seeking the exclusive right to show them. Initially, a film is available only in cinemas. A few months later airlines and hotel pay-per-view services get their shot. Then, about a year after a film is first released, it goes to a subscription service such as HBO or Sky, which has paid billions for the exclusive rights to broadcast about half of the films released by major Hollywood studios. When a film is shown on the network, it gets pulled from every other source, including à la carte streaming services, although it is often available for sale on Blu-Ray and DVD and via the venues that still rent movies on those media. (This is why the Netflix DVD service had a much better selection than the streaming service.)

It often takes five to seven years for a movie to get to the point that it goes to a service like Netflix, which offers a single monthly fee to stream all the content you like. As those licensing deals are already in place, there is not much the service can do about it. So Netflix and Amazon have been competing over long-term exclusive rights to old TV shows, which often get more popular as they age. All of these deals mean you can't subscribe to one service and feel satisfied with your selection, and no one is expecting this to change any time soon. If you want the instant gratification of having every show and film available to you at the push of a button, you will have to subscribe to multiple services, or spend a lot of time at friends' houses.

Just remember, it has been only a few decades since home video became available at all. There was a time when you could watch only what one of three major television networks decided to broadcast at a given time and films ran in the cinema and then disappeared. Fragmentation is annoying, but the amount of entertainment now available to us without our leaving the house is quite amazing. Focus on that while you are scrolling through all of those menu screens. Maybe it will help.

T

**Average perceived
allowable distance
for perfume to carry**

8 feet

TOO MUCH PERFUME:
THE EMPLOYEE WITH THE
SCENT CLOUD IN YOUR FACE

See also *Standing Too Close*.

Your colleague is intelligent, witty and has a pleasant personality, but you can't stand to be anywhere near her. The gallons of floral scent she bathes in make you sneeze, make your eyes water and generally offend your nose. It's perfume to her; it's odour to you.

Your co-worker's excess is an invasion of your personal space. We mentally allow a person about 2m (8ft) of space in public places. If their fragrance wafts past that line, it is now in our space. In recent years, people with offended noses have fought back by adopting scent-free policies, banning perfume and scented deodorants. These actions are

T

most common at schools and universities. Supporters of the zones argue that the smell is not just intrusive, but dangerous to people who have multiple chemical sensitivity (MCS). Victims of the disorder have become overloaded by environmental chemicals so their immune systems overreact to them.

MCS is controversial. While some doctors specialize in its treatment, others believe it is psychosomatic, or doubt it exists at all. The American Medical Association, the American Academy of Allergy and Immunology, the International Society of Regulatory Toxicology and Pharmacology and the American College of Physicians do not recognize it.

The problem with scent-free zones is that they tend to ban anything that has a smell rather than focusing on the chemicals themselves, which would tend to support the idea that it is more a question of personal space invasion than a concern over allergic reactions. You perceive smell when your nose senses traces of chemicals in the air and it conveys the message to the brain. The brain lets you know if the fragrance is pleasant or unpleasant. It doesn't always correspond to the danger level of the chemical. Natural gas is odourless; newly mown grass is fragrant.

The $42-billion perfume industry produces at least one hundred new scents each year. The simplest fragrance might have up to one hundred different ingredients. More complex – and more expensive – scents can have several hundred. It is estimated that there are between 5,000 and 6,000 commercially produced fragrances in the world.

Many in the environmental movement are specific in their grievances and want only chemically synthesized perfumes banned. Certain perfume ingredients, they say, are toxic and cause cancer.

Issues of health aside, there are good reasons why you might not like a specific perfume and why you feel so strongly about it. The sensory nerves in the nose are connected to the temporal lobe of the brain where memory is stored, and are closely tied to the limbic region, which is responsible for the most basic impulses – appetite, fear and sex. Whatever you feel about that perfume, you're going to have strong emotions about it.

In fact, scientists have recently discovered that some of the information we get from the nose does not register in the brain as smell at all but directly as emotion. Researchers from the University of Utah discovered that the vermeronasal organ in humans, a pair of pits in the nostrils, signals the brain when they detect certain substances. When these organs were signalling, the subjects were not consciously aware of a smell but reported a feeling of well-being. So when you smell that perfume, you may well be reacting at a level you cannot consciously appreciate.

Scientists no longer believe that there is a single human 'pheromone' that drives members of the opposite sex wild. Yet scent may play a bigger role in attraction than was previously believed and, interestingly, it is related not to sex hormones but to the immune system. Whenever the body is invaded by an alien body (a virus, bacteria, an implanted organ), the immune system attaches protein identifiers to it and creates antibodies specifically designed to combat it. A segment of our DNA, the major histocompatibility complex (MHC), 'remembers' this information and codes for it.

Researchers have discovered that women rate the smells of men whose MHC profiles were different from their own sexier than those whose MHC codes were similar. They theorize that we sniff out mates whose immunities are different from our own so as to produce stronger, healthier babies – the kids would be born with resistance to more diseases. A study by evolutionary ecologists Manfred Milinsky and Claus Wedekind found that participants with the same MHC types tended to prefer similar scents for their own use, but disliked the idea of the smells on a partner. They concluded that people select a perfume that amplifies the natural signal produced by their immune system so it accentuates their natural odour. If you don't like your co-worker's perfume, blame it on evolution.

TROLLS

See also *Unfriended*.

'Learn how to spell before you post @#$% comments you @#$% idiot. I get so fed up with morons like you wasting everybody's time. Why don't you @#$% and give your keyboard to someone with opposable thumbs.'

Why can't we just enjoy that YouTube video or blog post without being bombarded with rude comments? Trolling has the dubious distinction of being the only aggravation in this book that is done with the express purpose of being annoying. Trolls are distinct from ordinary abrasive people who start flame wars because they're in a bad mood and someone's political post rubbed them the wrong way. Those people can ruin your day, but they did not go online to bug you. Trolls do.

So why do people log on just to be obnoxious? Research has

concluded what you already guessed: they're bored. They're starved for attention. They want revenge. Also, they might be sadists. Erin Buckels and her team at the University of Manitoba found a strong correlation between people who say they enjoy trolling and personality traits that fall in what is called the Dark Tetrad: Machiavellianism, narcissism, psychopathy and sadism. They know they are hurting others, and that is the whole point. The more negative the reaction, the more fun it is. A 2012 study at Nottingham Trent University found that trolling increases the perpetrator's self-esteem, even as it erodes that of its targets.

Most of these young men – yes, they are mostly young men – would not dream of walking up to someone on the high street or in a supermarket and hurling insults. Fortunately for their antisocial pleasure, and unfortunately for the rest of us, the Internet provides what psychologists call a 'disinhibition effect'. That is to say, the anonymity of the online world, and not communicating face-to-face in real time, strip away social inhibitions.

Only 5.6 per cent of Buckels's survey respondents actually said that they enjoyed trolling, but it takes only one guest to pee in the punch bowl to make the whole thing unpotable. A Pew Research Center survey published in 2014 found that 70 per cent of 18-to-24-year-old Internet users had experienced harassment, and 26 per cent of women in that demographic had been stalked online. Trolls are shaping our online discourse. They stifle the voices of people who might feel vulnerable such as women and minorities. Beyond that, they subtly influence opinions and make our culture more polarized.

A team of researchers from the George Mason University Center for Climate Change Communication had people read a blog post containing a balanced discussion of the pros and cons of nanotechnology. Everyone read the same article; all that changed was the content of the comments. Some of them had civil discussions; others were filled with insults.

They discovered that when the comments were rude it pushed people's emotional buttons and made them retreat to their corners ready to fight. Those who came into the study with a pre-existing favourable view of nanotechnology became even more positive and those who came in with a negative view became more negative than the participants with the less emotional comments. Fighting words make us defensive and are not conducive to a rational and nuanced exchange of ideas. News sites have been trying to combat this but, as a staffer from Jezebel put it, 'It's like playing Whac-a-Mole with a sociopathic Hydra.'

If you have ever been the target of the hydra, you know that the anxiety and psychological symptoms can be just as strong as they would be if someone abused you 'in real life'. Replying in kind only fuels them, so for now the best advice the experts can give on dealing with these vermin is summed up in the cliché 'Don't feed the trolls'.

T

UNFRIENDED ▶ UNSOLICITED BULK EMAIL

UNFRIENDED

You were secretly infatuated with him all through secondary
school, and giggled every time you talked to him in the lunch
queue. You were over the moon when he agreed to be your
Facebook friend, but after a while it seemed as though you
hadn't seen one of his posts in a long time. You check your list of friends
and find that he is no longer listed. He has unfriended you. The nerve!
Then you decide you never really liked him anyway. What a loser.

Sometime between the first edition of this book and today, 'friend'
became a verb. Friends have always come and gone, but thanks to
social media the ebb and flow of friendship is documented. A person
has to make a conscious effort to unfriend you, and even though you
are not notified, chances are if you are more invested in the friendship

than the other person, you will, at some point, notice that your friend has absented himself from your list.

You might think that such a virtual rejection would be less painful than the old-fashioned face-to-face kind. You would be wrong. Numerous studies have shown that being dumped on a social network has all of the psychological impact of any other rejection. Neuroscience researchers have found that even minor exclusions, from mundane things like games of catch, can activate regions of the brain associated with physical pain. A 2013 study conducted at the University of Colorado Denver Business School found that 40 per cent of those surveyed said they would avoid someone in real life who had unfriended them on Facebook.

Of course, not all friendships are created equal whether online or off. Most of the people in your friends list are not what you might call intimates. Anthropologists suggest that a human being is capable of maintaining no more than 150 meaningful relationships. If you have 300 Facebook friends, you have probably accepted friend requests from your postman and a friend of a friend you met once at a party three years ago. 'Friends' who are most likely to be dumped on social networks are friends from school, back when you were thrown together and hadn't developed your own likes and political opinions. (Political differences are one of the main reasons people hide or drop friends on social networks.)

There are certainly people in your list who you would not notice at all if they disappeared. You are that person on someone else's list. The problem comes, online as elsewhere in life, when your idea of your level of friendship does not match the view of the other person. There is no way around it, when a person you thought was a friend turns out to be an acquaintance or less, it hurts. But you do not have to suffer.

Psychological studies have shown that the best way to get over the pain of rejection is to stop trying to figure out what went wrong and to reconnect with people who do love you. Talking about the pain of being unfriended with your remaining friends helps.

U

UNMATCHED SOCKS

Y ou start out with a drawer full of nice pairs of matched socks. Eventually, the order degrades to the point that you are forced to go to work wearing one white sock and one blue sock. What happened? Where the lost socks go is one of the great mysteries of the universe, but Robert Matthews, a visiting research fellow at Aston University in Birmingham, has investigated the results. His conclusion, published in *Mathematics Today*, is that, if your socks do go missing, you are indeed more likely to end up with unmatched socks than pairs.

Other blue
sock lost
in dryer

Blue sock

White sock

U

Here's how it works, when you lose one sock, it leaves behind its former partner. If you lose another sock, it could be the unmatched one (how great would that be). But there are many more paired socks than single socks, so it is probable that the next sock you lose will not be the matchless one. Because you are less likely to wear and wash the unmatched sock, leaving it safe and sound in the drawer where it is unlikely to be lost, the odds are even greater that the next sock to go will be part of a pair. Using a series of complex sock equations, Matthews concluded that, if socks are randomly lost from a drawer initially stocked with ten complete, but distinct, sock pairs, it is over one hundred times more likely that the result will be the worst possible outcome, with four complete pairs and six odd socks in the drawer, than the best outcome with seven complete pairs left.

'Drawing two socks at random even from a drawer full of complete pairs is most likely to produce nothing but two odd socks,' he writes. 'Thus, even if we have judiciously cleared out all the odd socks from our drawer we are still likely to have to rummage through a substantial fraction of the remaining socks before getting just one matching pair.' Of course, you increase the chances of pulling out matching socks if you buy only one kind. Matthews thought that was a bit drastic. He decided to limit his own sock purchases to two types, eight pairs of each. He learned, however, that Murphy's Law cannot be broken. After the sock gremlins struck, he returned to the shop only to discover that one of the styles had been discontinued.

U

UNSOLICITED BULK EMAIL, AKA SPAM

Unsolicited bulk email got its nickname from a sketch on the television programme *Monty Python's Flying Circus* in which everything on the menu came with Spam. The inbox of your email program is similar – spam, spam, message from your mum, spam, business correspondence and spam.

The folks at Hormel, makers of the canned meat product, Spam, aren't thrilled at the association with bulk email, by the way. Yet they have pretty much given up and accepted that we are not going to change our moniker for the annoying messages. Their lawyers, instead, concentrate their energies on making sure people don't capitalize the word 'spam' when referring to email and keeping pictures of the meat off web pages about Internet spam.

The good news about spam, the electronic kind, is that it has fallen to its lowest level in more than a decade. The bad news is that you are getting less spam because the 'Nigerian princes' have moved on from email scams to programming malware to steal your passwords and money directly. As spam has decreased, malicious software has increased. Some of the plain old marketing spam has also moved to your social network.

We really hate spam. A study conducted by the University of Georgia in 2006 compared our annoyance with spam versus junk mail and we hate our intrusive email more than those uninvited mailers. The study's authors speculate that this is because unwanted mail doesn't seem to thwart your efforts to see new messages the way downloading unwanted email does.

There may be less of spam today, but there is still a lot of it. Symantec reported in 2015 that 49.7 per cent of the email it scans contains spam. The 100 billion spam messages sent per day is not exactly what you would call a small volume. Then there is the solicited, but not really welcome, mass of messages like subscriptions to lists you haven't bothered to cancel, and social network notifications about random cat videos your acquaintances posted.

If your inbox gets on your nerves now, be grateful that we do not yet have some of the spam innovations that the experts are predicting, such as bots that are so good at mimicking human interaction that they fool you into thinking they are your friends. Or how about this nightmare scenario envisioned by Kristoffer Gansing, the artistic director of the Transmediale Festival for digital art and culture: 'With 3D-printing technology becoming more widely available, I can imagine a new kind of physical spam becoming possible,' he told the *Independent,* 'spamming people's workplaces and private lives with unwanted objects.'

U

VENDING MACHINES

STEP 1	STEP 2	STEP 3
INSERT BILL FACE UP	INSERT BILL FACE UP	Repeat Steps 1 & 2 indefinitely.

VENDING MACHINES SPITTING OUT YOUR MONEY

A pound doesn't go as far as it used to. Fortunately, technology has advanced to the point that machines can read paper money. Unfortunately, technology has not advanced to the point that it can always read paper money. Unless you have been living in a cave for the past 20 years, chances are you have had the experience of watching a perfectly good £5 note slide in and out of a machine accompanied by a distinctive 'zzzziipp'. Why is it that one machine will accept a wrinkled note and another won't? As the computer people say, 'It's not a bug, it's a feature.'

Vending machines, ticket machines and self-service tills are designed so that their owners can make money. They can't make money if the machine is easily fooled by counterfeit cash and pound-note-shaped photocopies. On the other hand, the vendor makes no money if you walk away without buying anything because the machine won't take your legal tender. So the manufacturers try to strike a balance between security and accepting mangled money. Coin Acceptors Inc. of St. Louis is one of the leading American manufacturers of the devices that read banknotes. They offer their vendors a choice of three levels of security. Those who put their machines in high traffic areas often opt for high security. A machine in an office might be safe with a lower level of security.

After a machine pulls the paper in, it scans it with light beams. The scanners are so sensitive they can tell what type of ink is used, what colour it is and what type of engravings appear. The highest level of security rejects banknotes with any imperfections, such as a torn corner. On the other hand, they can also be set so that they will take banknotes that have been slightly torn, splattered with food, soaked in water or written on with a pen. Even the most forgiving setting, however, can be fooled by a banknote that is too crumpled. The folds distort the image on the face.

Another possibility is that the machine has not been cleaned regularly and a build-up of money grime on the scanners is to blame. The best advice if a machine rejects your money is to change it in for a new banknote. If you can't do that, walk away. Don't try to rock the machine to get a free chocolate bar – you could get seriously hurt. On average, two people are crushed to death each year by toppling vending machines.

V

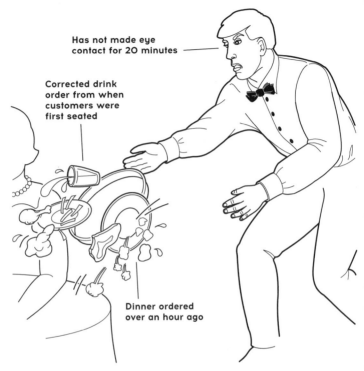

Has not made eye contact for 20 minutes

Corrected drink order from when customers were first seated

Dinner ordered over an hour ago

WAITERS

See also *What Did I Come in Here For?*

You are already fidgety and annoyed at having to wait half an hour to get a table at Chez Bob. You had even called to make a reservation. Charlie, your waiter for this evening, leans on the back of an empty chair as he takes your order. For a moment, you hesitate between ordering the chicken and the fish. 'I can come back,' he says and disappears. Ten minutes later he returns, takes your order, but comes back with the wrong drinks. Once again, he sprints away before you can call his attention to the error. Charlie steadfastly refuses to make eye contact, and although he passes close

W

to your table three times, he appears to have absolutely no hearing or peripheral vision.

When he brings your meals, you finally have a chance to mention your drink order. He takes your drinks away, promising to return with fresh ones. Time passes. He returns only when you are deep in conversation and interrupts you mid-sentence to ask, 'How is everything this evening?' 'Well, we don't have any drinks!' you snap. He rolls his eyes as if to say, 'What a rude customer.' By the time Charlie returns with the right drinks, three out of four of your guests have finished their meals. Charlie starts clearing the plates of all of them, including the one who has not finished. You decide not to risk dessert. Finally, Charlie returns with the bill and hands it to the only male at the table. He then disappears into a vast waitperson void as his tip dwindles from 15 per cent, to 10 per cent, to 5 per cent . . . Finally, you take the bill to the front of the restaurant and ask who you can pay. As you leave, you hear Charlie complain loudly that he got stiffed on his tip.

Have waiting staff got worse in the past few years? Probably. A strong economy gave us a boom in restaurants; meanwhile, employees had more options. They could pick and choose their jobs. This led to a shortage of qualified waiters and waitresses. 'We joke that pretty soon the chef is going to have to yell: "OK, table number five, come and get your food",' said one New Jersey restauranteur.

According to restaurant critic Tim Zagat, women get the worst restaurant service because there is an assumption that women, as a group, do not tip. There is also an assumption that a man at the table is paying. Waiters and waitresses alike tend to put the bill down in front of a man, even if a woman is the hostess.

In some countries, waiting tables is considered to be a highly skilled enterprise. There are highly regarded schools in Europe to train waiters. Not so in the United States. There, waiting tables is more often seen as something students and out-of-work actors do. Restaurants don't want to invest in a great deal of training if the employees aren't going to stick around. Waiters who do take pride in their profession are valuable and rare enough that they end up at the top restaurants, not Chez Bob.

W

According to the US National Waiters Association, a good waiter should check on the diner once in the first 90 seconds after the meal is put down on the table. He should then keep the diners in view and pay attention, but should not interrupt with questions like 'How is your food?' The waiter should never clear the plates until the slowest diner is finished. If the bill is delivered to the table, it should be set in the centre, not in front of any one diner unless requested. And, of course, payment should be picked up promptly.

At Chez Bob, waiters are paid less than minimum wage and they have to split their tips with the kitchen staff. Chez Bob is always understaffed and Charlie was recently hired. His previous job was washing windows. He was thrown into the deep end and always feels a little out of his element. Today, his colleague Annie called in sick and he is covering her tables as well as his own. One of the customers in her section is a regular who orders food for an invisible friend and shouts at the waiter if he doesn't bring it and set it at perfect right angles. All of his customers are annoyed to begin with because Bob insists on overbooking. Many people make reservations, don't show up and never call to cancel. If everyone does show up, there is not enough room for them all. That means long waits for everyone and short tempers all around. Charlie is keeping track of so many little things that they often get erased from his short-term memory before he has a chance to process them. Because he is overwhelmed, he is easily irritated by things – including you. Charlie does not lack peripheral vision – he is ignoring you because he isn't ready to deal with your table just yet.

And the time when waiters seem most apt to get lost? After they bring the bill. Mentally, they have stopped worrying about you because your meal is done. It is easier to forget to pick up the bill and bring change than it is to ignore someone waving his arm shouting, 'Waiter! I ordered soup an hour ago!'

W

WEATHER

See also *Potholes, Public Transport.*

The British, in a stereotype recognized the world over, are obsessed with the weather. This is because British weather is so relentlessly changeable – so aggravatingly difficult to predict. In Singapore in November you can be sure that it will start to pour around noon, but you will be back beside the swimming pool by four; in Barbados you can be reasonably confident that it won't rain from February to April, and the temperature will hover round the mid-twenties Celsius (about 75°F). In winter in Berlin you can predict that the temperature will skulk below 5°C (41°F) for three months, with plenty of rain and snow and no more than two hours' sunshine a day: it may be cold and miserable, but at least you know.

But Britain is an island, and it sits between the Atlantic Ocean and the large landmass of continental Europe. Not only that, but in the sky above lies the alarmingly named Polar Front of Convergence. The combination of these factors means that there is a lot of activity going on up there. No fewer than five air masses come Britain's way, bringing all sorts of weather. When two of them converge, they do battle about which is going to give way to the other, and the winner dictates what the weather conditions are going to be. Then another air mass comes along, picks another fight and – guess what? – that lovely morning that you thought was ideal for a picnic turns into a chilly, showery, cursing retreat into the nearest teashop.

As if this wasn't bad enough, about 10km (6 miles) up there is the jet stream. This is like an incredibly fast wind, and it doesn't blow in a straight line. Sometimes it sends Arctic air further south than normal, bringing unseasonal snow to the British Isles; sometimes it brings warm air further north, giving us heat waves or surprisingly mild winters. You just can't tell.

Despite these variables, statisticians come up with some pretty specific facts: intense hailstorms, for example, occur almost exclusively

W

between May and September, with a noticeable peak in July. The position of the jet stream in late June and early July tends to determine weather patterns for several weeks, explaining why the belief that if it rains on St Swithun's Day (15 July) it will rain every day for the next 40 days holds true a good 70 per cent of the time.

So have we really anything to complain about? OK, those rained-off picnics are a pain, but look at it another way. Manchester has a reputation for raininess, with at least 1mm of rain falling on 140 days a year on average. But if you travel west on the same line of latitude, you will eventually hit Saskatoon, which has rain on 157 days; due south, you will find that Bilbao (in sunny Spain!) has rain on 172 days. Manchester's average summer temperature is an unexciting 15–16°C (59–61°F), but in winter it is 4.5–7°C (40–44°F). True, you'll get more of a tan in summer in both Bilbao and Saskatoon, but in winter the Saskatoon temperature may not rise about 0°C (32°F) for four months and in Bilbao it won't beat Manchester by more than a degree or so. Maybe you're perfectly well off in northern England after all. But don't forget your umbrella. And take a jacket, just in case.

'WHAT DID I COME IN HERE FOR?' OR DESTINESIA

See also *What is that Word?*

It is like there's a force field between your bedroom and living room. You get up off the sofa, propelled by a desire to get something. You pass through the door and poof!, your memory is gone. What am I doing in this room? I know I came in here for something.

You are not going insane, you just have insufficient RAM at this time. Your short-term, or 'working', memory, is analogous to the RAM on your computer. It is temporary storage of information you need to keep in your head while you perform tasks that require that information.

There is a lot of information out there for the brain to process. You are not aware of much of the information your senses relay to the brain. While you are reading this, you are probably not thinking about your tongue. When your attention is brought to your tongue, however, you become aware of how it feels rubbing against that rough tooth in the back of your mouth.

That information was always there, but the brain was filtering it out. More than 99 per cent of the sensory information that comes in is deemed irrelevant by the brain and it is not encoded into long-term memory. Some information needs to be in your consciousness just long enough for you to act on it – a decision to go into another room, for example.

'The first law of memory, in terms of cognitive processes is that in order to remember something – encode something in the brain – you have to pay attention to it,' says Dr Sonia Lupien, a neuropsychologist at Douglas Hospital in Montréal, Canada, who specializes in the effects of stress on memory. 'Many times when we "forget" these little things, it's not even forgetting. It's not having encoded it in the first place.'

Usually, we do not concentrate on one task at a time. Our attention is divided. When you were sitting on the sofa contemplating a trip into the bedroom, you were also thinking about what to make for dinner, whether the kids had done their homework and how long it would be before your favourite show came on TV.

'Because we cannot put everything into our memory, we decide what is relevant and should be encoded and what is not,' Lupien says. 'The more things you do at the same time, the less you are going to be able to say this one is relevant, this one is not. The probability that it doesn't even get in will explain why, when you get to the room, you have no idea why you went there.'

The reason older people seem to experience this more often is that many of the things their minds used to give priority to now fall into the less relevant category. 'If before it was important to know where your glasses were because you had four minutes to leave the house, you unconsciously would say "Here they are. I know they are here. This is important." However, once you retire you have all the time in the world. Unconsciously it's not as important to find your glasses in 0.22 seconds. So you will not process this information in the same way.'

Want to be sure to remember why you went into the room? Put it higher on your list of priorities.

W

WHAT DOES IT REALLY COST? HIDDEN FEES

P eople hate it when their favourite brands raise their prices. Corporations know this, so they have to come up with a way to cover rising costs, or provide increasing returns to shareholders, while making it appear that they haven't raised their prices. Increasingly, they have done this through sleight of hand by tacking on hidden fees or taking aspects of a service that were once included and setting them aside as premiums, available for an added fee. They call this 'unbundling'.

In January 2017 the US National Economic Council released a report blasting airlines and hotels for hidden fees that drive up the costs of their products and services. 'When pricing is unclear, it threatens the competitive process by which consumers make decisions,' the report said. Of course, you discovered that without the Council's help when you went to check into that $26 Las Vegas hotel room only to find that 'resort fees' disclosed in the small print ran your bill up to $90. With most people carrying their own mobile phones, additional fees to use the landline in your room have mostly disappeared. But £1.50 'safe fees' (for having a safe in your room) have become common.

The most obvious case is in the airline industry. Since the airlines do nothing much to differentiate their brands in our minds, they have all joined in a race to the bottom, first eliminating meals, then snacks, then free films, then the little blankets, then checked bags. Instead of giving you these things, they charge you an à la carte fee after you have paid for your ticket. It generally doesn't make your flight cheaper; it just makes it seem cheaper, and hopefully it seems cheaper than the other airlines' offerings. Unbundling was unleashed in 2007 when airlines started to separately monetize everything that was not fuel or fuselage. This led to the 2009 Reuters headline 'U.S. Airlines Might Have Reached Limit on New Fees', but Reuters underestimated their creativity.

Recently, airlines discovered that they had trained their customers not to check bags any more, and the 'ancillary revenue' from checked bags

W

had dropped to a dangerously low level. So some airlines started charging for carry-ons. This was followed by the practice of making the advance reservation of a seat a premium service. The US Senate Commerce Committee, in 2015, after a review of seven different airline websites, found that 'consumers do not generally receive prominent disclosures regarding these fees when procuring airfare'. The fees are usually found in small print under headers like 'fare rules' or 'optional services'.

The lack of amenities has created its own set of annoyances, not the least of which is not actually knowing how much your holiday will cost. There is also the fact that more people are bringing their own meals onto flights that do not provide them. This bothers the neighbours who are tied into an uncomfortably small space beside someone with a tuna and garlic sandwich. A recent survey by GO Airport Express found that almost half of respondents said it was rude to carry on food with a strong odour. So don't do that.

Airlines and hotels are not the only companies that have tacked on fees for things they once offered for free. Prepaid gift cards can come with a whole host of fees including swipe fees, activation fees, reloading fees and fees for not using the card by a certain time.

Even retail products can be made to seem artificially cheaper by redesigning product packaging. The shelf price remains the same, but the amount of product you get is reduced. Have you noticed that your peanut butter jar is now dented inwards at the bottom? It holds a few grams less than it used to. Boxes of breakfast cereal are the same height they have always been, and look the same on the shelf. But the depth has shrunk, decreasing the box's volume. Your toilet paper still says it has 1,000 sheets, but the sheets have become a bit shorter. The gaps between the classic triangles in a Toblerone bar have increased while the total weight has decreased.

W   Of course, it does a company no good to alienate its customers. If unexpected hidden costs make us fume, why do they do it? The answer, according to Harvard professor David Laibson and Xavier Gabaix of the Massachusetts Institute of Technology, seems to be that it only makes some of us fume, and that is good enough to keep things profitable. They divide the consumer world into two categories: 'sophisticates' and 'myopes'. The sophisticates are good at comparison shopping, paying attention to the fine print and finding ways to avoid hidden fees. Myopes take advertised prices at face value and don't pay much attention to the final bill.

Businesses like the latter group because they can extract a bit of extra money from them from time to time. Now, if they were to start advertising that they treat their customers fairly, unlike their competitors who include hidden fees, they have not given the sophisticates any new information. They already did the work to find out what the lowest price is, fees and all. All they have done, therefore, is alert the myopes and transform some of them into sophisticates. Businesses don't want a bunch of sophisticates – they spend less money. If you create more sophisticates, you make people more conscious of spending everywhere, including at your hotel or airline. Thus, Laibson and Gabaix conclude, 'Neither firm has an incentive to do it.' You are left with only two choices: become a sophisticate or expect to pay more than you expected.

WHAT IS THAT WORD?

See also *'What Did I Come in Here For?'*

I went to the shops because I wanted . . . I had a recipe that called for . . . You know, one of those green things . . . it's not a cantaloupe. It's a vegetable, you know . . . It's . . . uurrrggghhh. It's green . . .

Psychologists call this a 'tip-of-the-tongue state'. You know a word, you use it regularly, but your brain refuses to access it. Studies show that people between the ages of 18 and 22 experience this state about once or twice a week. Those between the ages of 65 and 75 lose words about twice as often. Sometimes a word pops into your mind in a few seconds. Sometimes it takes days.

In the past, researchers speculated that the problem stemmed from a common word blocking a word that was similar to it. More recent studies suggest that people have the hardest time recalling a word like 'duplicate' which is less common and sounds like few other words. Apparently, the brain needs a bigger push to ferret out words we use less frequently.

Finding a word is actually a two-stage process. First the brain accesses the concept and then it searches for the sound of the word to match the meaning. Something similar happens when you see a familiar face but you can't recall the person's name. Distinct nerve cell circuits serve the part of the brain that stores the visual information and another processes the word – the person's name.

Often people remember the first letter of the word or name, or a similar-sounding word comes to mind. According to Deborah M Burke, a psychology professor at Pomona College in Claremont, California, people are twice as likely to find the word if they read or hear something that shares some of the missing word's sounds.

A Dutch researcher, Willem Levelt of the Max Planck Institute for Psycholinguistics, used advanced brain-imaging technology to solve the problem. He likens tip-of-the-tongue to a traffic jam of the brain. He says the harder you try to find the word, the harder it becomes. Most people have had the experience of remembering the word an hour after the relevant conversation ended. It just 'pops up'. So far, the experts do not know why. What they can tell you . . . Cucumber. That's the word I was looking for. Cucumber.

WORRY

Worry seems like preparation, but it is not. To prepare for something you have to do something. Most people prefer worry because it is much easier. You can do it sitting in your chair or in the shower or even lying in bed at night – especially lying in bed at night. It even feels kind of responsible, 'See, I'm not ignoring the problem, I'm worrying about it.'

Of course, worry is nothing new (in 1907, the English physician Caleb Williams Saleeby published a book with the title *Worry, the Disease of the Age*) and it will probably never go away. The same wonderful aspect of the brain that permits us to daydream and plan for the future also causes us to imagine worst-case scenarios. We are creative beings, which means that we are by nature problem-solving creatures. If we don't have a present problem to occupy our consciousness, a future one will do nicely.

In Shakespeare's day, when Hamlet spoke about 'apprehension', he meant something else entirely. 'What a piece of work is a man! How noble in reason! . . . in apprehension how like a god!' Back then, apprehension simply meant understanding. Now, four centuries later, it has taken on the tinge of anxiety. How did such a shift happen? I don't know, but I'm not going to worry about it too much.

When we envision bad things that are yet to happen, our 'fight-or-flight' responses kick in. Since the things we fear have not yet happened, and may never happen, we can't really fight them so we try to flee them, but where do you go to flee your imagination? We end up frozen, with nothing to do but worry more.

For example, creativity researcher Teresa Amabile of the Harvard Business School, studied a 6,000-person division in a global electronics company during the course of a 25 per cent downsizing. If you have ever worked for a company undergoing such a process, her findings will not surprise you. As people worried about their security, they disengaged from the work. Every measure of creativity in the work environment went down significantly and it stayed down more than five months after the

W

downsizing ended. Worrying about a potential job loss was more painful and draining for most than the job loss itself.

Worrying has little to do with your circumstances and everything to do with your proclivity to worry. Dr Tony Bates, a clinical psychologist, told the *Irish Times* that some people prefer to worry about the future so they don't have to deal with the present. 'We may also worry so as not to think about what's really bothering us,' he said. 'When our minds are dominated by worry, our memories and emotions become temporarily suppressed as the body prepares to deal with some imminent threat. Worrying about unlikely dangers may allow us to avoid thinking about the current issues that are undermining our sense of safety in the present.'

By the way, a team of researchers at Concordia University in Montréal, Canada, examined people's perceptions of gender roles and worry and compared these perceptions to how worried men and women actually reported themselves to be. Participants believed that women would be more worried about relationships and men would worry more about achievement and finances; they were wrong. In fact, the researchers discovered that while women were slightly more prone to worry about relationships they also tended to report more worry about achievement than men did. Women, various studies seem to indicate, worry more than men in general.

British stress expert Roger Henderson recently published a study on what he calls 'money sickness syndrome', which is debt stress that can be so severe it leads to skin rashes, shortness of breath, nausea, irritability, an inability to concentrate and heart palpitations. One in five couples in the study had such severe money worry that it affected their love life. Again, women were especially likely to report a loss of libido due to worry.

A study undertaken by researchers at Purdue University, Lafayette, Indiana in 2007 seems to confirm that worry can kill you. The 12-year study of 1,663 men between the ages of 43 and 91 revealed that the subjects who were the most neurotic, that is, inclined to worry over relatively minor setbacks, were 40 per cent more likely to die during the study. This does not bode well for Woody Allen.

W

Since worry was the 'disease of the age' at the turn of the last century, let's see what they had to say about it at the time. Writing in 1919, George Lincoln Walton, author of *Why Worry?* (you didn't know they had self-help books back then, did you?), wrote: 'I cannot expect to be wholly immune from the misfortunes of mankind . . . If we fret about the weather it is because of an insistent desire that the weather shall conform to our idea of its seasonableness . . . Suppose now, instead of devoting all our attention to the weather we should reason somewhat as follows: As long as I live on this particular planet, I shall be subject perhaps three days out of four, to atmospheric conditions which do not suit me. Is it worth my while to fret during those three days and to make it up by being elated on the fourth? . . . Or, as someone has said, why not "make friends with the weather?" If one will cultivate this frame of mind he will be surprised to find that a certain physical relief will follow.'

This chimes with what Dr Ethel Quayle, a lecturer at University College Cork, Ireland, had to say about worry: don't worry about it. 'The more we worry about the detrimental effects of worrying, the more of a problematic state it becomes,' she told the *Irish Times*. 'The very process of trying to control private events, like thoughts, makes us hypersensitive to having them and is an increasing source of worry itself.'

W

XMAS FOR CHRISTMAS

X = CHI

XMAS FOR CHRISTMAS

Merry Xmas. It's meant as a festive greeting, but to many the 'X' is a big irritant. Some dislike it because it's inelegant and not the way people speak. Others find it aggravating for religious reasons. 'Since someone mentioned that using "Xmas" is taking the "Christ" out of Christmas, I have never written "Xmas",' wrote a *Calgary Sun* reader. 'Maybe a weird little hang-up, but working in reverse, every time I see the word "Xmas" it's a little reminder to me that Christ belongs in Christmas!'

It may seem that Xmas is a symbol of our modern, secularized, commercialized, 'I wanna video drone' Christmas. (By the way, while we're on the subject of seasonal irritants, it seems that a selfie stick with a microphone for portable karaoke was one of the hot gifts recently.) The spelling 'Xmas', however, dates back to the 16th century. The X is a stand-in for the Greek letter *chi*, which resembles our X. The name of Christ in Greek was *Xristos*, thus *chi* represented Christ. Its shape was also reminiscent of the cross. For these two reasons, *chi* was used regularly in religious contexts. The 9th-century *Book of Kells* contains a lavishly decorated chi-rho page. In the 16th century, the use of Xmas spread throughout Europe along with such spellings as 'Xren' for 'christen' and 'Xtian' for 'Christian'. Christians of that time would, therefore, immediately recognize the 'Christ' in 'Xmas'. We no longer do. Xmas is easier to fit into headlines and advertisements, however, which contributes to the modern perception that it is an attempt to secularize the festival.

As for that other winter festive spelling problem – Hanukkah, Hanuka, Chanukah . . . which is it? The answer is . . . it depends. The word for the Jewish festival is translated from Hebrew, which has a different alphabet. When linguists translate from a language that has a different set of characters, they try to approximate the sound with the letters of the second language as best they can. Hanukkah literally means 'dedication'. It refers to the rededication of the Temple in Jerusalem after it had been defiled by the Syrians. The first letter of the word is the Hebrew *het*, which is pronounced like the 'ch' in the Scottish word loch. German, and thus the German-influenced Yiddish, pronounce the 'ch' similarly, unlike in English where we would tend to see 'ch' and pronounce it as in 'chalk'. Originally, the name of the festival was transcribed Chanukkah. Because English speakers tended to pronounce Chanukkah incorrectly, the spelling evolved to begin with an 'h', which is a better English approximation. We still don't pronounce it quite right, but at least we get closer than when we try to pronounce it with a 'ch'.

As for the middle of the word and the one 'k' or two question Hebrew has two letters that correspond to our 'k', *kaf* and *kof*. Hanukkah uses *kaf*, which has a stronger 'k' sound. For that reason, it is often translated as a double 'k', but there aren't many words with a double 'k' in English, thus, the double 'k' doesn't convey much meaning to us and it is often dropped. As for the 'h' at the end, it doesn't change the sound of 'ah' and it is sometimes dropped. The most frequent variations you will see are Hanukkah or Chanukah.

X

YELLOW SPOTS ▶ YOUR CALL IS IMPORTANT

YELLOW SPOTS ON PUBLIC TOILET SEATS, OR IF YOU SPRINKLE WHILE YOU TINKLE . . .

See also *Toilet Seat Left Up*.

So you think men's toilets are dirtier and grimier than women's? You're wrong. Dr Charles Gerba, an Arizona microbiologist, has made a career of studying the places where germs lurk. As it turns out, women's facilities tend to have more harmful germs than men's. The researcher guesses this is because more children use them, putting the blame on young boys with bad aim.

There is another possibility. Women's toilets have more bacteria because women use them. To avoid sitting on a dirty public toilet seat, many women squat or hover just above the bowl. It is not an easy task and they often miss the mark leaving drips and splashes on the seat.

The number of yellow drops has been increasing in public toilet stalls. It is a problem that builds upon itself. The more women feel they are unsanitary, the more likely they are to hover. According to one study (yes, of course people study this), about 59 per cent of women now relieve themselves in this manner.

Let's dispel a few myths. You can't catch venereal disease from toilet seats. To put it as delicately as possible, the parts of the anatomy that would carry sexually transmitted diseases do not actually come into contact with the toilet seat. As Gerba told a Salon reporter, 'You don't catch things off your butt. You catch things off your hands.'

In the course of his research, Gerba learned that only one out of fifty-nine public toilet seats has *E. coli* bacteria on it. He found much more bacteria on the sinks. Another study three years later revealed that the kitchen is much germier than the average bathroom. There are more than 200 times more faecal bacteria on a chopping board (from raw meat) than on the home toilet seat. 'If you have a choice between

Y

licking a toilet seat or a cutting [chopping] board, go with the toilet seat,' Gerba said.

The biggest danger from toilet seats is actually from injury, not disease. Between 2002 and 2010 there were 13,175 injuries related to the toilet or toilet seat. As with most categories of injury, the bulk of these are from slipping and cracking various body parts on them. There is another significant form of toilet injury, however, and it mostly involves young boys. Falling toilet seats injure about one hundred boys a year. The majority of these crush incidents are painful and embarrassing but not serious or long-lasting . . . but I digress.

A simple solution to the tinkle-sprinkle problem is for women to do what men do. No, I don't mean standing to pee. Boys learn, early on, to lift the toilet seat to avoid hosing it. If women do not want to sit on the seat, there is no reason why they should not lift it as well.

Y

59 per cent of
women do not
sit on toilet seat
while urinating.

Y

'YOUR CALL IS IMPORTANT TO US': ON HOLD

My call is not important to you! If my call were so important to you, you would answer it! An item from the 'I could have told you that for free' file: a study conducted for Prudential Insurance of America found that 41 per cent of Americans surveyed grew 'angrier and angrier by the minute' when put on hold. What else drives us crazy? I'll give you a hint:

'Yes.'
'Something else.'
'Agent.'
'Agent!'

Yes, it is voice recognition technology. We hate shouting at robots so much that most people only call customer service after they have exhausted all other avenues. The first place most people go to get answers is the company's web page. By the time you have given in and

Y

picked up the phone, it is unlikely that your question is common enough to be part of a phone tree and having to wade through a menu of options that don't fit is one of life's little frustrations.

The silver lining is that companies are trying to use the dreaded technology to reduce your irritation. It doesn't help them to have disgruntled customers. One way they entertain you while you are on hold, surprisingly enough, is to bombard you with commercials. We complain about them, but, in spite of what we say, messages on hold keep us on the line. A Nationwide Insurance study shows that on-hold messaging reduces hang-ups by 50 to 80 per cent. In fact, 15 to 35 per cent of callers responded to the advertising messages and bought additional items.

Companies have also been experimenting with hold music. Karen Niven, a lecturer at Manchester Business School, studied the effects of different types of music on customers' moods. The results were published in the *Journal of Applied Social Psychology* in 2014. Niven guessed that popular music with pro-social lyrics, like Michael Jackson's 'Heal the World' would make people most cooperative and happy. She tested the hypothesis by changing the music at a call centre to play standard pop music, pro-social pop music or instrumental music. The results surprised Niven. The callers who listened to pop music were less angry than those who had heard the instrumental 'lift music', but they were equally annoyed by the pro-social music. It seems the contrast between healing the world and being placed on hold got their dander up. If pop music makes us happy, why don't more companies use it? Licensing fees.

The good news is that voice-recognition systems are getting smarter, and most are programmed to detect anger and frustration. In a lot of systems, you will be transferred to a human being if you shout a few choice words into the receiver.

Thank you for continuing to hold. Your call is important to us. Please hold for a message from our sponsor . . .

Y

ZIPS

Fabric caught
in teeth of zip

Shirt tail

ZIPS AND FLIES, STUCK

The metal-toothed clothing fastener dates back to 1891 and a Chicago inventor named Whitcomb Judson. It wasn't until 1917 that a Swedish engineer named Gideon Sunback updated the design so it resembled the fastener we know today as a zip. The American word 'zipper' began life as a trade name. The BF Goodrich company marketed a model of galoshes with a hookless fastener. The brand name of the shoes was soon applied to their new-fangled fastener. As zippers gained popularity, more were able to experience the joys of having a zip stick at an inopportune moment.

If you take a close look at a zip – to avoid misunderstandings you should probably make it your own – you will see that it is made up of a slider with a pull that runs over two rows of moulded metal or plastic teeth, which are shaped in such a way that they interlock. Most often, it

Z

is the slider that breaks down. If you find your zip just won't zip, or if it has the unfortunate habit of leaving you exposed to the public, the slider is probably worn or bent out of shape. Ditto if it seems welded in place. A common way for sliders to become bent is fabric that gets caught in the zip's teeth. Pull the thread out of the zip. If you still can't get the thing open, you can try greasing the zip with crayons, candles, soap or lip balm. Once you get the offending item off, you can fix the slider by gently squeezing it back into shape with a pair of pliers. 'Gently' is the active word here. You want to squeeze it just enough to keep it from sliding down the teeth or open it just enough to move freely, not enough to seal it shut or break it in half. If the zip is missing teeth or it is coming off the fabric all together, this is more complicated. If you can sew, you can fix it. If you can't, call a tailor.

While we're on the subject of stuck zips, briefly, here's what *Men's Health* has to say about getting stuck in your zip. While it is extremely rare that anyone gets his entire member stuck, like the boy in the movie *There's Something About Mary*, minor mishaps do happen. Zip accidents usually result in superficial skin injuries but they are still painful enough to make number three on the magazine's list of the '8 Worst Things You Can Do to Your Privates'. Contrary to popular belief, most zip injuries occur when unzipping, not zipping. If you find yourself in this position, *Men's Health* advises you pull the zip in the direction it came from in one swift motion. Then assess the damage and, if necessary, apply a bandage to stop the bleeding.

INDEX

A

academic language 16–17

acne 18–19

advertisements
  pop-up ads 151–2
  spam emails 220–1

aircraft
  armrests 26–7
  ears popping 80–1
  motion sickness 134–5
  seats 20–2

airline fees 233–5

alarms: car alarms 42–3

ants 24–5

apologies 139–41

armrests 26–7

B

bad breath 23, 29–30

beer, flat 87–8

biscuits, dunking 31–2

brain freeze 110–11

buffering 35–7

bureaucracy 38–40

C

cables, undersea 173–4

cars
  car alarms 42–3
  child seats 46–7
  parking 44–5
  potholes 153–4
  road rage 165–7
  slow drivers 171–2
  speeding tickets 186–8
  stereos 33–4
  tailgating 172
  theft 43
  traffic jams 195–6

cats, scratching 48–9

chewing gum 50–1

children
  child seats 46–7
  reading to 52–3

Christmas 242–3

clickwrap 54–6

clingfilm 57

coffee
  dunking biscuits 31–2
  rings 59
  spilling 58–9

colds 60–1

computers
  buffering 35–7
  click-through 54–6
  dust on monitors 77–8
  keyboard crud 122–3
  passwords 148–50
  pop-up ads 151–2